3

TESTAMENT

COLLEGEVILLE BIBLE COMMENTARY

ISAIAH

John J. Collins

THE LITURGICAL PRESS

Collegeville, Minnesota

ABBREVIATIONS

Gen—Genesis
Exod—Exodus
Lev—Leviticus
Num—Numbers
Deut—Deuteronomy
Josh—Joshua
Judg—Judges
Ruth—Ruth
1 Sam—1 Samuel
2 Sam—2 Samuel
1 Kgs—1 Kings
2 Kgs—2 Kings
1 Chr—1 Chronicles
2 Chr—2 Chronicles
Ezra—Ezra
Neh—Nehemiah
Tob—Tobit
Jdt—Judith
Esth—Esther
1 Macc—1 Maccabees
2 Macc—2 Maccabees
Job—Job
Ps(s)—Psalm(s)
Prov—Proverbs

Eccl—Ecclesiastes
Song—Song of Songs
Wis—Wisdom
Sir—Sirach
Isa—Isaiah
Jer—Jeremiah
Lam—Lamentations
Bar—Baruch
Ezek—Ezekiel
Dan—Daniel
Hos—Hosea
Joel—Joel
Amos—Amos
Obad—Obadiah
Jonah—Jonah
Mic—Micah
Nah—Nahum
Hab—Habakkuk
Zeph—Zephaniah
Hag—Haggai
Zech—Zechariah
Mal—Malachi
Matt—Matthew
Mark—Mark
Luke—Luke

John—John
Acts—Acts
Rom—Romans
1 Cor—1 Corinthians
2 Cor—2 Corinthians
Gal—Galatians
Eph—Ephesians
Phil—Philippians
Col—Colossians
1 Thess—1 Thessalonians
2 Thess—2 Thessalonians
1 Tim—1 Timothy
2 Tim—2 Timothy
Titus—Titus
Phlm—Philemon
Heb—Hebrews
Jas—James
1 Pet—1 Peter
2 Pet—2 Peter
1 John—1 John
2 John—2 John
3 John—3 John
Jude—Jude
Rev—Revelation

Nihil obstat: Robert C. Harren, J.C.L., *Censor deputatus.*

Imprimatur: ✛ George H. Speltz, D.D., Bishop of St. Cloud. January 16, 1986.

ISBN 0-8146-1420-5 (volume 13 O.T.); ISBN 0-8146-1394-2 (complete set O.T.)

Library of Congress Cataloging in Publication Data
Collins, John Joseph, 1946–
    Isaiah.
    (Collegeville Bible Commentary. Old Testament ; 13)
    Includes the complete biblical text of Isaiah from the New American Bible.
    1. Bible. O.T. Isaiah—Commentaries. I. Bible. O.T. Isaiah. English. New American. 1986. II. Title. III. Series.
BS1515.3.C65 1986   224'.107'7   86-7306
ISBN 0-8146-1420-5 (pbk.)

Cover: "In the desert prepare the way of the Lord! Make straight in the wasteland a highway for our God!" (Isa 40:3). Road to the Timnah Valley. *Photo by Richard T. Nowitz.*

CONTENTS

The Book of Isaiah

Introduction

The Book of Isaiah presents in a particularly acute way two problems that confront the Christian interpreter of the Old Testament. The first concerns the discrepancy between the surface impression of the text and modern critical reconstructions of its history and meaning. Christian tradition, like Jewish tradition, long regarded the entire book as the work of a single prophet, Isaiah of Jerusalem. Critical scholarship, however, has taught us to distinguish First Isaiah (chs. 1–39), Second Isaiah (chs. 40–55) and Third Isaiah (chs. 56–66). Second and Third Isaiah are now dated to the late sixth century B.C.E., two hundred years after Isaiah of Jerusalem. Moreover, it now appears that less than half of First Isaiah actually contains words of the prophet himself. The remainder was added by anonymous scribes over several hundred years. Jewish legend had it that the prophet Isaiah met his death by being sawn asunder during the reign of the impious King Manasseh. Some conservative Christians have felt that his book has suffered a like fate at the hands of the critics.

The second problem concerns the Christological interpretation of the Old Testament. The Book of Isaiah has been treasured by Christians because it seems to predict crucial elements in the life of Jesus; the most striking examples are the virgin birth in Isa 7 and the passion and death in Isa 53. The book is cited or alluded to more than three hundred times in the New Testament. Jesus himself claimed to fulfill a text from Isaiah (61:1–2) in his sermon at Nazareth (Luke 4:18). Yet, critical scholarship has insisted that we must first understand the biblical texts in their own historical context. Isaiah had a message for the people of his own time, and this message did not require foreknowledge of events that would happen several hundred years later. The use of Isaiah by the Gospel writers tells us about the faith of the early Christians rather than the prophet's own message.

Critical scholarship, then, has cast doubt on the unity of the Book of Isaiah and on the Christian belief that it predicts Christ. Both these points have been shocking for Christians, although the shock has worn off, except in very conservative circles. Yet, the critical approach to the Bible should not be seen as a negative development. It has enriched our understanding of the Scriptures by showing how "the word of the Lord" is rooted in and speaks to concrete historical situations. The Bible is not a book of dogmatic propositions to be learned and believed, but a moving illustration of the faith of a people in ever-changing circumstances. If we know how an oracle conveyed its message in its original setting, we then have a guide to the way it should be understood in other settings. We cannot fully appreciate Matthew's use of the Immanuel prophecy (Matt 1:23) unless we understand the message Isaiah was delivering to King Ahaz when he originally spoke it (Isa 7:10-17).

For those who have mastered it, historical criticism has been a tremendously liberating force, for it has brought to light many aspects of biblical faith that had been submerged by the dogmatic theology of a later age. We now recognize, however, that a purely historical approach is also limited. In the case of Isaiah, we simply do not know the historical setting of some oracles, or we know it only in a very general way. Besides, the power of some passages lies in the fact that they transcend their original situations; they express fundamental hopes, fears, or insights that are applicable in recurring situations. The great messianic prophecies of Isaiah fall into this category. A passage like Isa 11, which dreams of a day when the wolf will lie down with the lamb, articulates a universal yearning for peace that is not peculiar to any historical situation. In this commentary we will try to do justice both to the historical particularity and to the universality of Isaiah's prophecies.

The composition of the book

Fundamental to the critical understanding of Isaiah is the insight that chapters 40–66 cannot be the work of Isaiah of Jerusalem but come from a much later time. Not only do these chapters *predict* the restoration of Jerusalem after the Babylonian Exile, but they *presuppose* the Exile itself. Second Isaiah *presupposes* that the Exile is already at an end. Third Isaiah (chs. 56–66) *presupposes* that the Jewish community has already returned to Judea. The issue, then, is not whether the prophet Isaiah could have predicted events of a much later time; the fact that the later events are presupposed is a sure indication of the time when these chapters were written.

Even within First Isaiah there is much material that was added later. Chapters 13–23 consist of oracles against various nations. Only a few passages in these chapters (for example, ch. 20) are likely to have come from the time of Isaiah himself. Chapters 24–27 constitute the so-called "Apocalypse of Isaiah." These chapters are no earlier than the Babylonian Exile and may even be later than Third Isaiah. Chapters 34–35 come from the sixth century, about the time of Second Isaiah. Finally, chapters 36–39 are taken, with very little modification, from 2 Kgs 18–20. The original oracles of Isaiah are found primarily in chapters 1–12 and 28–33 (plus a few passages in chapters 13–23). Even these chapters have come to us through the hands of editors who left their mark by the arrangement of the material and by minor inser-

ns. (Most of the editorial work can be placed after the Exile, but some
ay have been associated with the reform of King Josiah in 621 B.C.E.) The
ok of Isaiah, then, is not a monograph by an individual author but the
llection of an ongoing tradition that spanned more than two hundred years.

e prophet Isaiah

At the origin of this tradition stands Isaiah of Jerusalem. The superscrip-
n in Isa 1:1 tells us that he prophesied "in the days of Uzziah, Jotham,
haz and Hezekiah, kings of Judah." The great vision in chapter 6, which
usually thought to mark the beginning of his prophetic activity, is dated
the year of Uzziah's death, probably 742 B.C.E. We know that he was ac-
ve late in Hezekiah's reign at the time of an Assyrian invasion in 701 B.C.E.
escribed in Isa 36–38). His career, then, spanned roughly the second half
the eighth century B.C.E. His contemporaries included the prophets Amos,
osea, and Micah.

Isaiah's career was marked by a series of crises caused by the military
croachment of the great superpower of the East, Assyria. The first great
isis, in the years 735–733 B.C.E., was the Syro-Ephraimite war. Syria joined
rces with the northern kingdom of Israel (Ephraim) to form an alliance
ainst the Assyrians. When King Ahaz of Judah refused to join, they
ounted a campaign against him with a view to deposing him and installing
more cooperative king. This was the occasion of Isaiah's famous Immanuel
rophecy. Ahaz appealed to Assyria for help. In 733 B.C.E. Samaria, the capi-
l of northern Israel, was forced to submit. Ahaz remained king in Jerusa-
m as a subject of Assyria.

The next great crisis came about a decade later. The northern kingdom
f Israel rebelled against Assyria, and in 722 B.C.E. Samaria was destroyed.
s population was deported and foreign settlers were brought in. The north-
rn kingdom of Israel ceased to exist. This catastrophe may be prophesied
Isa 28:1-4.

Judah was again in danger in 713 B.C.E., when the Philistine city of Ash-
od rebelled against the Assyrians. Isa 20 records the activity of Isaiah on
his occasion.

Finally, in 701 B.C.E., Hezekiah of Judah revolted and provoked the fa-
ous campaign of Sennacherib. Most of the southern kingdom was ravaged.
he Assyrian king boasted that he shut up Hezekiah in Jerusalem "like a bird
a cage." Yet Jerusalem was not destroyed, and Hezekiah remained on the
rone. The prose account in Isa 36–38 attributes the deliverance of Jerusa-
m to "the angel of the Lord" (37:36).

This succession of crises plays some part in the ordering of the material
First Isaiah. Chapters 6–8, which are widely thought to be a memoir from

Isaiah himself (see 8:16), clearly belong to the early period. Some material in chapters 10–23 can be attributed to the middle period, between 722 and 701 B.C.E. The oracles in chapters 28–32 relate to the time of Sennacherib. Some scholars think that the oracles in chapters 2–5, which deal primarily with social abuses, belong to the earliest period of the prophet's activity, before the Syro-Ephraimite war, at a time when Amos was making similar charges in northern Israel, but there is no clear evidence of their date.

The politics of Isaiah

Isaiah's preaching is directly concerned with the events of the day. He denounces the luxury of those who join house to house and field to field and of the women who parade in jewelry. His ideal seems to be the simple way of life in which people can live on curds and honey, the natural produce of the land. He does not see the loss of the vineyards—a source of wealth and luxury—as a great catastrophe. He certainly does not urge his people to fight to defend them; rather, he advocates a quietistic, pacifistic stance in the face of the Assyrian threat.

Isaiah's ideal of social simplicity was not conceived in rustic isolation. He was an urban prophet familiar with the temple (ch. 6). He had access to the king as a kind of political advisor, both in the early days of the Syro-Ephraimite war and in the time of Sennacherib at the end of his career. He was an educated man, as we can see from his mastery of Hebrew verse and from his familiarity with international politics. His social and political vision did not arise from naïveté but from his fundamental theological convictions.

Theological principles

At the heart of Isaiah's prophecy is his vision of God as "the Holy One of Israel," which is presented most vividly in chapter 6. The holiness of God shows up the inherent sinfulness of humanity. The power of the spirit contrasts with the powerless flesh (Isa 31). The emphasis on God's holiness is rooted in the praise of God's glory in the temple cult (compare Psalms 29, 93, 96–99). For Isaiah, the exaltation of God is the corollary of human finitude. Human pretensions to power are pathetic and doomed to failure. Consequently, Isaiah is very critical of the attempts of the Judean kings to play power politics or even to control their own destinies. He is in conflict with the sages, the professional advisers of the king, whose plans are overridden by the "plan of the Holy One of Israel" (5:19).

The central demand of Isaiah is for faith in this God. "Unless your faith is firm," he tells Ahaz, "you shall not be firm!" (7:9). Faith here means trust and reliance on God rather than on one's own resources. The context for this faith is provided by the royal ideology of the Davidic house. The divine charter of the dynasty is provided by the oracle of Nathan to David, recorded in 2 Sam 7. There the Lord promises David:

> I will establish a house for you. . . . I will raise up your heir after you, sprung from your loins, and I will make his kingdom firm. . . . And I will make his royal throne firm forever. I will be a father to him, and he shall be a son to me. And if he does wrong, I will correct him with the rod of men and with human chastisements; but I will not withdraw my favor from him as I withdrew it from your predecessor Saul, whom I removed from my presence. Your house and your kingdom shall endure forever before me; your throne shall stand firm forever (2 Sam 7:11-16).

One of the terms used to express the "firmness" of the dynasty is derived from the same root as the word for "faith."

The promise to David is the basis for a theology of kingship found in the psalms. The essential points are found in Psalm 2. If the kings of the earth rise up against the Lord and "his anointed" (the king), God will laugh at them, for "I myself have set up my king on Zion, my holy mountain" (Ps 2:6). The decree of the Lord is then proclaimed: "You are my son; this day I have begotten you" (Ps 2:7). This special father-son relationship is reaffirmed in Psalm 110, where the king is invited to "Sit at my right hand till I make your enemies your footstool" (Ps 110:1). The king can even be addressed as "God" (Ps 45:7), although he is clearly subordinate to the God who blesses him. The king is hailed as God's representative without reservation.

This glorification of the monarchy presumes certain responsibilities. The king is supposed to act "in the cause of truth and for the sake of justice" (Ps 45:5), to defend the afflicted and crush the oppressor (Ps 72). The whole ideology assumes and demands a very high degree of trust and reverence for the kingship (compare also Pss 89, 132).

Trust in the kingship goes hand in hand with trust in Mount Zion, the site of the temple in Jerusalem, as the dwelling place of God. Later Jewish theology might qualify the idea that God actually lived in the temple (1 Kgs 8:27; compare Isa 66:1; Acts 7:48), but Psalm 46 declares that it is "the holy dwelling of the Most High. God is in its midst; it shall not be disturbed" (Ps 46:5-6). The people of Jerusalem need not fear, "though the earth be shaken," because "the Lord of hosts is with [them]" (Ps 46:3, 8; compare Psalm 48). The worshiper in the temple could hope to see God's power and glory (see Ps 63:3), as indeed Isaiah does (Isa 6). The rhetoric of the temple worship, then, proclaims that the people need fear no adversary, because they have God's presence in their temple and God's support for their king.

This theology of kingship and temple provides the context for Isaiah's faith. (Unlike his contemporaries Amos and Hosea, Isaiah does not draw upon the tradition of the Exodus.) Isaiah demands that king and people alike live by the faith they profess. But this was not so easy when the Assyrian army was at the door. Isaiah is not so naive as to think that God will obligingly protect the people from all harm. He recognizes the extent of the suffering and destruction that will be inflicted, but he insists that life will go on. God will leave the people a remnant.

This theme of Isaiah's message, proclaimed in the name of his son Shear-jashub ("A remnant shall return," 7:3), is at once both good news and bad news. The remnant will ensure the survival of the people, but only after widespread destruction; it will be like the survival of a stump when a tree has been cut down. From this stump will come an ideal ruler in a future time (ch. 11), and Mount Zion will be exalted as a center for all peoples in days to come (ch. 2).

The ideal king and ideal temple are future ideals for Isaiah. They highlight the shortcomings of the present rulers and present cult. Isaiah affirms his faith in the royal theology but prevents it from serving as political propaganda for the kings of his day.

The political theology of Isaiah uses the popular traditions in an ironic way. The irony is best captured in the symbolic name Immanuel. "God is with us" was the professed faith of the Davidic line. For Isaiah, however, this is not a guarantee of easy salvation. The presence of God can be mediated by the sword of the Assyrian, the rod of Yahweh's anger (10:5). Salvation, for Isaiah, is not identical with wealth and prosperity, but with the purified worship of God. The people might, ironically, be better off when reduced to a remnant, stripped of their vineyards and forced to rely on curds and honey like the first Israelites.

Isaiah's quietistic stance goes hand in hand with his social criticism. The people who tried to survive by alliances with Egypt or who relied on horses, the armaments of their day (Isa 31), were the same people who joined house to house and field to field and got drunk on the produce of their vineyards. These were the people who stood to gain from national independence, who had something to fight for. Ironically, Judah and Israel were vulnerable to Assyrian greed because they had a measure of wealth and luxury. If they lived the simpler life, without wealth or power, they would be left in peace. The ideal kingdom sketched in Isa 11 is not a powerful empire, but one of peace and simplicity.

We can appreciate why the early Christians saw correspondences between Isaiah's prophecies and the kingdom proclaimed by Jesus. Two thousand years later Isaiah's political ideals have lost none of their relevance to the issues of international politics and the welfare of society.

Second Isaiah

The prophet we know as Second Isaiah worked in a very different situation. In the early years of the sixth century B.C.E., the kingdom of Judah had finally collapsed. In 586 B.C.E. Jerusalem was destroyed by the Babylonians. King Zedekiah had seen his sons slain before his eyes and was then blinded and taken in fetters to Babylon with the leaders of his people. The Jewish people were decimated, and the survivors humiliated. Some Jews saw this catastrophe as a punishment for their sins, but many must have wondered whether their God enjoyed any control over the course of events at all.

Then hope came from an unexpected quarter. The Persian king Cyrus entered Babylon as conqueror in 539 B.C.E. Within a year he had authorized the Jewish exiles to return home. This decree was consistent with Cyrus' generally tolerant policies toward subject peoples. He presented himself to the Babylonians as a liberator who was granted his triumph by the god of the Babylonians, Marduk. To the Jews he proclaimed that it was the Lord, the God of heaven, who had sent him, and that the Lord had also charged him to rebuild the temple in Jerusalem (so Ezra 1:1-4). Second Isaiah, elated at the unexpected deliverance, gladly proclaimed that Cyrus was the anointed ("messiah") of Yahweh (Isa 45:1).

The oracles of Second Isaiah are written in celebration of this deliverance and attempt to reformulate the faith of Israel in light of it. They consist of short hymnic units. It is not clear whether they have been arranged in a deliberate order. Chapter 40 is certainly an introduction to the collection and establishes several of its main themes. Some scholars find a shift at chapter 49. Chapters 49–55 are somewhat more sober in tone than chapters 40–48. They abandon some characteristic themes of the earlier chapters, such as the polemic against idolatry and disputes with the Babylonians. The later chapters show a strong interest in Zion. The differences, however, do not lead us to suppose that chapters 49–55 have a setting different from that of chapters 40–48. All these oracles were delivered after the rise of Cyrus and before the practical problems of the restoration had become apparent. They were probably written in Babylon.

Four of the short poems that make up Second Isaiah are commonly set apart as the "Servant Songs": Isa 42:1-4; 49:1-6; 50:4-9; 52:13–53:12. These passages are distinguished by their focus on the figure called "the Servant of Yahweh." Scholars of an earlier generation thought that these oracles were the work of a different prophet, but that view is now widely rejected. It is also doubtful whether they even represent a distinct, late stage in the composition of the book, as is sometimes claimed. Rather, they should be seen as an integral part of the collection that makes up Second Isaiah and interpreted in that context.

Theological themes

Second Isaiah, no less than Isaiah of Jerusalem, celebrates the transcendent power of God, before whom all flesh is like grass. He relates this to two distinctive themes.

First, Yahweh, God of Israel, is the Creator of all, the first and last, and there is no God besides Yahweh. Second Isaiah affirms that Yahweh alone is God in a more emphatic manner than any other biblical writer. Earlier biblical writers admit the existence of other gods but forbid the Israelites to worship them. Even Second Isaiah does not deny the existence of Babylonian gods (for example, Bel and Nebo—46:1), but he views them as helpless idols that have no power to save, and so they are in effect "no-gods." The monotheism of Second Isaiah is the basis for his highly sarcastic polemic against the worship of idols. All nations are obligated to serve Yahweh, since Yahweh is Creator of all.

Second, this Creator-God is the redeemer of Israel who buys it back from a state of slavery. This theme is based on the idea that Yahweh is bound to Israel by bonds of kinship. It also goes hand in hand with the prophet's view that the liberation from Babylon is a new Exodus.

The theme of the new Exodus is introduced already in 40:3: "In the desert prepare the way of the Lord!" The prophet is not interested in the Exodus as ancient history but as the myth or paradigm that reveals what God is like in the present. Yahweh is a God who liberates slaves, who overturns the status quo. Yahweh is a hidden God (45:15) whose ways may be obscure for a time but who will then be revealed in unexpected ways.

Undoubtedly the best known theme of Second Isaiah is the portrayal of the figure of the Suffering Servant, especially in the great Servant Song of Isa 53. This passage has attracted much attention because it has traditionally been taken as a prophecy of the passion of Jesus, and indeed it played some part in the early Christian understanding of Jesus' death. The original significance of this figure for the Jews of the sixth century is still in dispute. The Servant has been identified with a wide range of historical figures from Moses to Zerubbabel (the governor at the time of the restoration and heir to the Davidic throne) or even the prophet himself. More probably, however, the Servant was not a historical individual but an idealized representation of the faithful Jews in exile.

The Servant poems, then, can be read as Second Isaiah's explanation of the Babylonian captivity. The view that the Jews were being punished for their sins is inadequate. They had received double for all their sins (40:2). Rather, their suffering had a positive purpose; they were to serve as a light to the nations. It was the infirmities of the other nations that they bore. Their lives were an offering for the sins of the Gentiles. Second Isaiah believed that the unexpected restoration of the Jews would bring the other nations to their senses and lead them to acknowledge Yahweh as the true God. In this he was disappointed, but the Suffering Servant persisted as a model of piety that has had profound influence on both Jewish and Christian spirituality.

Third Isaiah

Isa 56–66 is closely related to Second Isaiah but comes from a slightly later period, after the exiles had returned to Jerusalem and discovered the harsh realities of the situation. Some of the oracles, especially chapters 60–62, still resound with the enthusiasm of Second Isaiah; other passages, however, attest to deep divisions within the postexilic community and a sense of near desperation on the part of the prophet (chs. 63–66). Yet, out of these circumstances emerged the powerful vision of a new heaven and a new earth (65:17) that would be picked up later by the author of the Book of Revelation in the New Testament. These chapters raise fundamental issues concerning the priorities of a community in difficult times and the nature of true worship.

The so-called "Apocalypse of Isaiah"

The oracles that were inserted into First Isaiah at chapters 24–27 resemble Third Isaiah in their sense of near desperation with the present and desire for a radically different future. They are called "the Apocalypse of Isaiah" because of their heavy reliance on mythological symbols, which is a well-known feature of apocalyptic literature. They are not cast in the particular form of an apocalypse, however, which is a supernatural revelation, usually a vision mediated by an angel (see Dan 7–12). These chapters are prophetic oracles from an unknown prophet. They are often thought to reflect the further deterioration of the postexilic community after the time of Third Isaiah, perhaps about 500 B.C.E. Some scholars put the date much later, even as late as 300 B.C.E.

The difficulty of establishing a firm date for these chapters in itself tells us something about their nature. The heavy reliance on mythical symbols has a generalizing effect. These oracles provide a cluster of metaphors for a recurring type of situation. (This is also true of some of the oracles against the nations in Isa 13–23.) The portrayal of cosmic devastation in Isa 24 is as apt in an age of ecological crisis and nuclear threat as it was at any time in the ancient world. The hope that God "will destroy death forever" and "wipe away the tears from all faces" (25:8) remains the ultimate human aspiration.

Within the Book of Isaiah these chapters form a conclusion to the oracles against the nations by moving away from particular denunciations to more general, cosmic descriptions of judgment and salvation.

The unity of Isaiah

It is easier to show that the various parts of the Book of Isaiah come from different periods than to provide an explanation as to why they were all combined under Isaiah's name. Some scholars are willing to suppose that it was sheer accident, that material copied on a single scroll came to be regarded as a single book. The more plausible suggestion is that the later writers considered themselves part of an Isaianic tradition. Despite the differences between the various sections, there are some basic themes that run throughout. These include:

—the centrality of the holy mountain of Zion;

—a reliance on mythical symbolism to express the hopes (and fears) for the future;

—a yearning for universal peace that involves not only Israel but the right ordering of all nations.

All these themes are related to the cult of the Jerusalem temple. It may be that the continuity of the Isaianic tradition is simply that it is a Jerusalem tradition and that "all the Isaiahs" drew on a tradition of cultic piety. We will find that this is true even when the prophets were sharply critical of current cultic practice, for example in Isa 1 and 66. There are also some indications that later "Isaianic" writers drew motifs and allusions from the earlier Isaianic corpus; for example, the oracle on the vineyard in Isa 27 builds on the "song of the vineyard" in chapter 5. In the "new creation" of Isa 65 the wolf and the lamb will graze together, as in the messianic prophecy of Isa 11.

The fondness for mythical symbolism and ideal representations throughout the Book of Isaiah has lent itself to reinterpretation by subsequent generations. The general character of the messianic prophecies allowed the early Christians to see their fulfillment in Jesus. This classical Christian reinterpretation of Isaiah should not, however, cause us to ignore the fundamental messages of these writings in their historical contexts; nor should it distract us from seeking analogies between the prophet's situation and our own or from asking how his religious ideals can be correlated with our modern problems.

The Book of Isaiah

Text and Commentary

A. THE BOOK OF JUDGMENT

I: INDICTMENT OF ISRAEL AND JUDAH

1 **Israel's Sinfulness.** ¹The vision which Isaiah, son of Amoz, had concerning Judah and Jerusalem in the days of Uzziah, Jotham, Ahaz and Hezekiah, kings of Judah:

²Hear, O heavens, and listen, O earth,
   for the LORD speaks:

Sons have I raised and reared,
   but they have disowned me!
³An ox knows its owner,
   and an ass, its master's manger;
But Israel does not know,
   my people has not understood.
⁴Ah! sinful nation, people laden with wickedness,
   evil race, corrupt children!
They have forsaken the LORD,
   spurned the Holy One of Israel,
   apostatized.

FIRST ISAIAH

Isa 1–39

INTRODUCTORY PROPHECY

Isa 1:1-31

The opening chapter singles out the themes of judgment and salvation, which are characteristic of the whole book. It contains some oracles of the original Isaiah but has been edited as an introduction to the collection of oracles. The editor probably wrote after the fall of Jerusalem in the sixth century B.C.E. His message is simple: Whatever disasters befell Jerusalem are a punishment for infidelity; but if the people repent and are obedient, they will again eat the good things of the land.

1:1 The superscription. The "vision" here refers to the entire revelation of Isaiah, most of which is in verbal form. The prophet's father, Amoz, should not be confused with the prophet Amos, whose career overlapped Isaiah's. The reigns of the kings listed cover most of the second half of the eighth century. If Isaiah's career began in the year of Uzziah's death, the probable dates are 742–701 B.C.E.

1:2-8 Judah devastated. The description of Zion, "left like a hut in a vineyard" (1:8), recalls the boast of the Assyrian king Sennacherib that he had shut up Hezekiah of Judah "like a bird in a cage," and may refer to the

⁵Where would you yet be struck,
    you that rebel again and again?
The whole head is sick,
    the whole heart faint.
⁶From the sole of the foot to the head
    there is no sound spot:
Wound and welt and gaping gash,
    not drained, or bandaged,
    or eased with salve.
⁷Your country is waste,
    your cities burnt with fire;
Your land before your eyes
    strangers devour
    [a waste, like Sodom overthrown]—
⁸And daughter Zion is left
    like a hut in a vineyard,
Like a shed in a melon patch,
    like a city blockaded.
⁹Unless the LORD of hosts
    had left us a scanty remnant,
We had become as Sodom,
    we should be like Gomorrah.
¹⁰Hear the word of the LORD,
    princes of Sodom!
Listen to the instruction of our God,
    people of Gomorrah!
¹¹What care I for the number of your
    sacrifices?
    says the LORD.
I have had enough of whole-burnt rams
    and fat of fatlings;
In the blood of calves, lambs and goats
    I find no pleasure.
¹²When you come in to visit me,
    who asks these things of you?
¹³Trample my courts no more!
    Bring no more worthless offerings;
    your incense is loathsome to me.
New moon and sabbath, calling of
    assemblies,
    octaves with wickedness: these
    I cannot bear.
¹⁴Your new moons and festivals I detest;
    they weigh me down, I tire of the
    load.
¹⁵When you spread out your hands,
    I close my eyes to you;
Though you pray the more,
    I will not listen.
Your hands are full of blood!

same situation in 701 B.C.E. Isaiah, however, does not put the blame on the Assyrians but on the Judeans themselves: "They have forsaken the Lord, spurned the Holy One of Israel" (1:4). The opening line, "Hear, O heavens, and listen, O earth" (1:2), introduces an indictment for breach of covenant in Deut 32:1. In this case, however, there is no appeal to the Sinai covenant or to the Exodus from Egypt. Instead, the prophet appeals to an instinctive natural law: if an ox and ass can know their master, then Israel should know its God and know what is right. The prophet's concern is not merely with the breach of specific laws but with the lack of a proper religious attitude that should inform all of life.

Verse 9 introduces the theme of the remnant. It is a small remnant, ensuring survival, but little more.

1:10-16 An oracle on true worship. This oracle begins with a mention of Sodom and Gomorrah, and is placed here because the same cities are mentioned in verse 9. Sodom and Gomorrah were the cities of the Plain, destroyed by fire from heaven because of their corruption (Gen 19). In verse 9 the analogy was with the total way in which they were destroyed. In verse 10 the Judean leaders are addressed as "princes of Sodom" because they are equally corrupt.

6 Wash yourselves clean!
Put away your misdeeds from before
    my eyes;
    cease doing evil; 17learn to do good.
Make justice your aim: redress the
    wronged,
    hear the orphan's plea, defend the
    widow.
18Come now, let us set things right,
    says the Lord:
Though your sins be like scarlet,
    they may become white as snow;
Though they be crimson red,
    they may become white as wool.
19If you are willing, and obey,
    you shall eat the good things of the
    land;
20But if you refuse and resist,
    the sword shall consume you:
    for the mouth of the Lord has spoken!
21How has she turned adulteress,
    the faithful city, so upright!
Justice used to lodge within her,
    but now, murderers.
22Your silver is turned to dross,
    your wine is mixed with water.
23Your princes are rebels
    and comrades of thieves;
Each one of them loves a bribe
    and looks for gifts.
The fatherless they defend not,
    and the widow's plea does not reach
    them.
24Now, therefore, says the Lord,
    the Lord of hosts, the Mighty One of
    Israel:
Ah! I will take vengeance on my foes
    and fully repay my enemies!
25I will turn my hand against you,
    and refine your dross in the furnace,
    removing all your alloy.
26I will restore your judges as at first,
    and your counselors as in the begin-
    ning;
After that you shall be called
    city of justice, faithful city.
27Zion shall be redeemed by judgment,
    and her repentant ones by justice.
28Rebels and sinners alike shall be
    crushed,

The theme of this oracle is true worship. God professes no pleasure in the constant sacrifice of animals or even with the observance of the new moon and sabbath, because "your hands are full of blood!" (1:15), not only because of the sacrifices but because of the violence of their lives. Isaiah is not opposed to ritual as such. He says they need a ritual of washing to symbolize repentance and purification. Ritual, however, is only as good as the intentions it expresses. What matters is how people treat the widows and orphans, not how often they go to the temple or offer sacrifice. A very similar critique of the cult and plea for justice is found in Amos 5:18-27, also from the eighth century B.C.E.

1:18-20 Call to repentance. This brief insertion has the tone of the law in Deuteronomy and expresses succinctly the message of the editor. Rather than just proclaim judgment or salvation, as the prophet typically does, it sets a goal for repentance and so emphasizes human responsibility. The assumption that obedience ensures prosperity is naive, however, and was sharply criticized in the later biblical tradition, most obviously in the Book of Job but also in Second Isaiah.

1:21-31 Redemption by judgment. The chapter concludes with a threat of punishment for political and social corruption. The main point to note

those who desert the LORD shall be consumed.

²⁹You shall be ashamed of the terebinths which you prized,
and blush for the groves which you chose.

³⁰You shall become like a tree with falling leaves,
like a garden that has no water.

³¹The strong man shall turn to tow,
and his work shall become a spark;
Both shall burn together,
and there shall be none to quench the flames.

2 **Zion, the Messianic Capital.** ¹This is what Isaiah, son of Amoz, saw concerning Judah and Jerusalem.

² In days to come,
The mountain of the LORD's house
shall be established as the highest mountain
and raised above the hills.
All nations shall stream toward it;
³ many peoples shall come and say:
"Come, let us climb the LORD's mountain,
to the house of the God of Jacob,
That he may instruct us in his ways,
and we may walk in his paths."
For from Zion shall go forth instruction,
and the word of the LORD from Jerusalem.

⁴He shall judge between the nations,

is that the punishment is seen as redemptive, like the refining of metals by fire. Zion will be purified. The experience will be severe, but it is necessary if the cherished claims to justice and faithfulness are to be rendered appropriate.

ORACLES AGAINST JERUSALEM AND JUDAH

Isa 2:1–12:6

These chapters are given a new introduction in 2:1 and gather oracles that are mainly from the early period of Isaiah's activity. We may distinguish the rather general social oracles of chapters 2–5, the memoir of Isaiah in chapters 6–8, the messianic oracles in chapters 9 and 11 (separated by oracles on Samaria and Assyria), and a concluding psalm in chapter 12, which may have marked the conclusion of a distinct collection.

2:2-5 The future of Mount Zion. Verses 2-4 are duplicated almost exactly in Mic 4:1-3. Micah, like Isaiah, was an eighth-century prophet of the southern kingdom. We do not know which prophet, if either, composed this oracle. The prospect of nations streaming to Mount Zion is often related to the pilgrimages of Jewish exiles to Jerusalem in the postexilic period. Even in the preexilic period, however, Mount Zion was considered to be a sacred mountain, the center of the earth, and important for the whole world (see Psalms 46–48).

In the lifetime of Isaiah, King Hezekiah is said to have tried to destroy the "high places" where people worshiped outside of Jerusalem and to cen-

and impose terms on many peoples.
They shall beat their swords into plow-
    shares
    and their spears into pruning hooks;
One nation shall not raise the sword
    against another,
    nor shall they train for war again.
⁵O house of Jacob, come,
    let us walk in the light of the Lord!

The Lord's Judgment against Idols

⁶You have abandoned your people,
    the house of Jacob,
Because they are filled with fortune-
    tellers
    and soothsayers, like the Philistines;
    they covenant with strangers.

⁷Their land is full of silver and gold,
    and there is no end to their treasures;
Their land is full of horses,
    and there is no end to their chariots.
⁸Their land is full of idols;
    they worship the works of their
    hands,
    that which their fingers have made.
⁹But man is abased,
    each one brought low.
    [Do not pardon them!]
¹⁰Get behind the rocks,
    hide in the dust,
From the terror of the Lord
    and the splendor of his majesty!
¹¹The haughty eyes of man will be
    lowered,

tralize the cult (2 Kgs 18; 2 Chr 31). Samaria and the northern kingdom had recently been destroyed, and Hezekiah was trying to rally the survivors to Jerusalem. Isa 2:2-5 would make good sense in this context. The "house of Jacob" that is invited to walk in the light of the Lord (v. 5) certainly includes the northern kingdom of Israel.

This vision of the future of Zion already contains the idea that Israel is a light to the nations, a theme we will meet again in Second Isaiah. The Israelites are not told to go out to convert the nations but to attract them by their worship on Zion. In the ideal world of the future time, all nations will come together to the central city of Jerusalem. Recognition of the claims of Jerusalem is the converse of recognition of Yahweh as sovereign. This recognition and the acceptance of Yahweh's instruction are seen as the keys to world peace, when swords will be beaten into ploughshares.

Whatever the origin of this oracle, it introduces themes we will meet repeatedly in the Book of Isaiah and is in harmony with the great messianic prophecy of Isa 11. We should note that the prophet Joel (Joel 4:10) inverts the great vision of peace and bids the nations beat their ploughshares into swords in anticipation of battle on the day of the Lord. Neither prophecy should be taken as a prediction of the future; both are projections of basic human hopes and fears.

2:6-22 The Day of the Lord. This long oracle begins by giving reasons why God has abandoned the people, the house of Jacob (probably the northern kingdom, which was conquered by the Assyrians in 733 B.C.E. and again decisively in 722 B.C.E.). The offenses include idolatry and pursuit of treasures and armaments. All are symptoms of human pride. In response,

the arrogance of men will be abased,
and the LORD alone will be exalted,
on that day.

¹²For the LORD of hosts will have his day
against all that is proud and arrogant,
all that is high, and it will be brought
low;

¹³Yes, against all the cedars of Lebanon
and all the oaks of Bashan,

¹⁴Against all the lofty mountains
and all the high hills,

¹⁵Against every lofty tower
and every fortified wall,

¹⁶Against all the ships of Tarshish
and all stately vessels.

¹⁷Human pride will be abased,
the arrogance of men brought low,
And the LORD alone will be exalted, on
that day.

¹⁸   The idols will perish forever.

¹⁹Men will go into caves in the rocks
and into holes in the earth,
From the terror of the LORD
and the splendor of his majesty,
when he arises to overawe the earth.

²⁰On that day men will throw to th
moles and the bats the idols of silver and
gold which they made for worship.

²¹They go into caverns in the rocks
and into crevices in the cliffs,
From the terror of the LORD
and the splendor of his majesty,
when he arises to overawe the earth

²²As for you, let man alone,
in whose nostrils is but a breath;
for what is he worth?

Judgment of Judah and Jerusalem

3 ¹The Lord, the LORD of hosts,
shall take away from Jerusalem and
from Judah
support and prop [all supplies o
bread and water]:

²Hero and warrior,
judge and prophet, fortuneteller and
elder,

³The captain of fifty and the nobleman
counselor, skilled magician, and ex
pert charmer.

God will manifest his majesty "on that day" (v. 11). The "Day of the Lord" is known from a famous passage in Amos 5:18-20. There it appears that most people look forward to the Day of the Lord, but Amos says that it will be "darkness and not light." Most probably it was a festival day (perhaps during the fall festival of Tabernacles) when God was supposed to be manifested to the cultic community.

Amos suggests that when God is really manifested, most people will not be able to endure it. Similarly, in Isaiah the "day" takes on the character of a battle day when God will rout any foes. The description of the divine manifestation echoes the cultic celebration of the psalms (for example, Psalms 29 and 97) and is related to the tradition of God's kingship. Isaiah is thinking not only of a theophany in the cult, however, but of an occasion when all will flee to caves from the terror of the Lord. It is possible that the terror will be conveyed through the Assyrian invasion, but Isaiah sees it as the manifestation of God. Humanity will then recognize its puny nature before the overwhelming power of God, and the folly of human ambitions to wealth and power will be exposed.

3:1-12 Anarchy in Jerusalem. "That day" will also have effect in Jerusalem. Isaiah sketches a breakdown of the social order. "Hero and warrior,"

will make striplings their princes;
  the fickle shall govern them,
And the people shall oppress one an-
    other,
  yes, every man his neighbor.
The child shall be bold toward the
    elder,
  and the base toward the honorable.
When a man seizes his brother
  in his father's house, saying,
"You have clothes! Be our ruler,
  and take in hand this ruin!"—
    Then shall he answer in that day:
"I will not undertake to cure this,
  when in my own house there is no
    bread or clothing!
  You shall not make me ruler of the
    people."
⁸Jerusalem is crumbling, Judah is fall-
    ing;
  for their speech and their deeds are
    before the LORD,
  a provocation in the sight of his
    majesty.
⁹Their very look bears witness against
    them;
  their sin like Sodom they vaunt,
They hide it not. Woe to them!
  they deal out evil to themselves.
¹⁰Happy the just, for it will be well with
    them,
  the fruit of their works they will eat.
¹¹Woe to the wicked man! All goes ill,

with the work of his hands he will
  be repaid.
¹²My people—a babe in arms will be
    their tyrant,
  and women will rule them!
O my people, your leaders mislead,
  they destroy the paths you should
    follow.
¹³The LORD rises to accuse,
  standing to try his people.
¹⁴The Lord enters into judgment
  with his people's elders and princes:
It is you who have devoured the
    vineyard;
  the loot wrested from the poor is in
    your houses.
¹⁵What do you mean by crushing my
    people,
  and grinding down the poor when
    they look to you?
  says the Lord, the GOD of hosts.
¹⁶The LORD said:
  Because the daughters of Zion are
    haughty,
  and walk with necks outstretched
Ogling and mincing as they go,
  their anklets tinkling with every step,
¹⁷The Lord shall cover the scalps of Zion's
    daughters with scabs,
  and the LORD shall bare their heads.

¹⁸On that day the LORD will do away with
the finery of the anklets, sunbursts, and

anyone who could lay claim to power is removed. The people will be ruled
by mere boys (v. 4), women, or even a babe in arms (v. 12). That "a little
child" should be leader may sound idyllic in Isa 11, but here (v. 5) it is a
symptom of chaos. There was no such breakdown of order in Isaiah's time.
The prophecy is partly a wish and partly an assertion that such a breakdown
could happen, and that the pride of the leaders has a shaky foundation.

3:13-15 The accusation. The formal accusation in verses 13-15 focuses
on one aspect of that foundation. The political leaders, the elders and princes,
have built their wealth by appropriating land and exploiting the poor. A similar theme is characteristic of Amos. We will meet it again in Isa 5.

3:16-4:1 The women of Jerusalem. Isaiah is especially severe on the
women. He provides an impressive inventory of their finery. He seems to
relish the prospect that their heads would be shaved and they would be led

21

crescents; ¹⁹the pendants, bracelets, and veils; ²⁰the headdresses, bangles, cinctures, perfume boxes, and amulets; ²¹the signet rings, and the nose rings; ²²the court dresses, wraps, cloaks, and purses; ²³the mirrors, linen tunics, turbans, and shawls.

²⁴Instead of perfume there will be stench,
   instead of the girdle, a rope,
And for the coiffure, baldness;
   for the rich gown, a sackcloth skirt.
   Then, instead of beauty:
²⁵Your men will fall by the sword,
   and your champions, in war;
²⁶Her gates will lament and mourn,
   as the city sits desolate on the ground.

4 ¹Seven women will take hold of one man
on that day, saying:
"We will eat our own food
   and wear our own clothing;
Only let your name be given us,
   put an end to our disgrace!"

The Messianic Branch

²   On that day,
The branch of the Lord will be luster
   and glory,

and the fruit of the earth will
   honor and splendor
   for the survivors of Israel.
³He who remains in Zion
   and he that is left in Jerusalem
Will be called holy:
   every one marked down for life
      Jerusalem.
⁴When the Lord washes away
   the filth of the daughters of Zion,
And purges Jerusalem's blood from he
   midst
   with a blast of searing judgment,
⁵Then will the Lord create,
   over the whole site of Mount Zio
   and over her place of assembly,
A smoking cloud by day
   and a light of flaming fire by nigh
⁶For over all, his glory will be shelte
   and protection:
   shade from the parching heat of day
   refuge and cover from storm an
      rain.

The Vineyard Song

5 ¹Let me now sing of my friend,
   my friend's song concerning h
   vineyard.

away in sackcloth by the Assyrians (they were not, but it was a distinct possibility). He treats the women as the representatives of the culture of luxury and pride, and therefore especially ripe for a fall. We find a similar attitude in Amos, who called the women of Samaria "cows of Bashan" (Amos 4:1).

4:2-6 The glorious remnant. The final oracle relating to "that day" is probably the work of a later editor. Elsewhere in Isaiah the remnant is not portrayed in such glorious terms. The signs of God's presence—the smoking cloud by day and the flaming fire by night—recall the Exodus tradition, which is also out of character for Isaiah. Yet the passage is developing a genuine theme of Isaiah: Jerusalem must be purged if it is to be holy, but the purge is ultimately the means to salvation.

The "branch of the Lord" here is a general reference to whatever God will cause to grow, synonymous with "the fruit of the earth." The same word is used for a messiah in Jer 23:5; Zech 3:8; 6:12.

5:1-7 The song of the vineyard. This famous poem is a parable, like Nathan's parable in 2 Sam 12 or some of the parables of Jesus. The speaker

My friend had a vineyard
  on a fertile hillside;
He spaded it, cleared it of stones,
  and planted the choicest vines;
Within it he built a watchtower,
  and hewed out a wine press.
Then he looked for the crop of grapes,
  but what it yielded was wild grapes.
Now, inhabitants of Jerusalem and men
  of Judah,
  judge between me and my vineyard:
What more was there to do for my
  vineyard
  that I had not done?
Why, when I looked for the crop of
  grapes,
  did it bring forth wild grapes?
⁵Now, I will let you know
  what I mean to do to my vineyard:

Take away its hedge, give it to grazing,
  break through its wall, let it be
  trampled!
⁶Yes, I will make it a ruin:
  it shall not be pruned or hoed,
  but overgrown with thorns and
  briers;
I will command the clouds
  not to send rain upon it.
⁷The vineyard of the LORD of hosts is
  the house of Israel,
  and the men of Judah are his cherished plant;
He looked for judgment, but see,
  bloodshed!
  for justice, but hark, the outcry!

Doom of the Unjust

⁸Woe to you who join house to house,

does not at first disclose his true subject but leads his listeners to pass judgment before they realize that they are condemning themselves. The vineyard involves a double allegory. On the one hand, there is the obvious agricultural sense of the words. On the other hand, the fact that the song is said to be a love song, sung for a friend, suggests that the friend's vineyard is really his wife. There is a hint, then, of marital infidelity as a second level in the allegory. The song is not very explicit about the sins of Israel, except that they involve bloodshed and injustice. The indictment draws its force from the analogy with the unproductive vineyard and the less obvious analogy with marital infidelity. It appears that both kingdoms, Israel and Judah, stand accused.

There is yet another nuance to the allegory. The vineyard was very valuable property that contributed greatly to the life of luxury. It symbolized the wealth of the land. The parable suggests that this wealth has not produced a just society. The threat that the vineyard would be overgrown by thorns and briers was fulfilled rather literally after the Assyrian invasions.

The entire poem may be compared to Hos 2, where God threatens to make the land a wilderness and the analogy with marital infidelity is again present. The vine is a favorite symbol for Israel in the Old Testament: compare Hos 10:1; Jer 2:21; Ezek 15:1-8; 19:10-14. Compare also the parable of the vineyard in the New Testament: Matt 21:33-42; Mark 12:1-10; Luke 20:9-18.

5:8-16 Denunciation of social abuses. These oracles are proclamations of woe and have a dirge-like effect. They do not invite the wicked to repent

who connect field with field,
Till no room remains, and you are left
    to dwell
    alone in the midst of the land!
⁹In my hearing the LORD of hosts has
    sworn:
    Many houses shall be in ruins,
    large ones and fine, with no one to
        live in them.
¹⁰Ten acres of vineyard
    shall yield but one liquid measure,
And a homer of seed
    shall yield but an ephah.
¹⁷Lambs shall graze there at pasture,
    and kids shall eat in the ruins of
        the rich.
¹¹Woe to those who demand strong
    drink
    as soon as they rise in the morning,
And linger into the night
    while wine inflames them!
¹²With harp and lyre, timbrel and flute,
    they feast on wine;
But what the LORD does, they regard
    not,
    the work of his hands they see not.
¹³Therefore my people go into exile,
    because they do not understand;
Their nobles die of hunger,
    and their masses are parched with
        thirst.

¹⁴Therefore the nether world enlarges
    throat
    and opens its maw without limit;
Down go their nobility and the
    masses,
    their throngs and their revelry.
¹⁵Men shall be abased, each one broug
    low,
    and the eyes of the haughty lowere
¹⁶But the LORD of hosts shall be exalte
    by his judgment,
    and God the Holy shall be show
        holy by his justice.
¹⁸Woe to those who tug at guilt wi
    cords of perversity,
    and at sin as if with cart ropes!
¹⁹To those who say, "Let him make has
    and speed his work, that we may s⟨
    it;
On with the plan of the Holy One ⟨
    Israel!
    let it come to pass, that we may kno
        it!"
²⁰Woe to those who call evil good, ar
    good evil,
    who change darkness into light, ar
    light into darkness,
    who change bitter into sweet, ar
    sweet into bitter!
²¹Woe to those who are wise in the
    own sight,

but are announced as certain and unavoidable. They paint a vivid pictur
of Israelite society in the eighth century. The large landowners add hous
to house by foreclosing on debtors or pressuring the smaller farmers off th
land (see the story of Naboth's vineyard in 1 Kgs 21). The large estates coul
then be turned into profitable vineyards, which supported the luxurious (an
drunken) lifestyle of the rich rather than supplying the staples of life for th
poor. Isaiah insists that those who exalt themselves in this way will b
humbled before the majesty of God.

5:17-25 Denunciation of the wise. Isaiah is especially angry at the profes
sional sages, the political advisers of their day. They are skilled in politica
rhetoric, call evil good and good evil. They indulge in petty corruption, ac
quitting the guilty for bribes. Besides, being "wise in their own sight
(v. 21), they do not allow for God's control of events or for the ability ⟨
a prophet to discern it. Isaiah insists that the "Holy One" has a plan, whic⟨

and prudent in their own esteem!
²²Woe to the champions at drinking wine,
    the valiant at mixing strong drink!
²³To those who acquit the guilty for
    bribes,
    and deprive the just man of his rights!
²⁴Therefore, as the tongue of fire licks
    up stubble,
    as dry grass shrivels in the flame,
Even so their root shall become rotten
    and their blossom scatter like dust;
For they have spurned the law of the
    LORD of hosts,
    and scorned the word of the Holy
    One of Israel.
²⁵Therefore the wrath of the LORD blazes
    against his people,
    he raises his hand to strike them;
When the mountains quake,
    their corpses shall be like refuse in
    the streets.
For all this, his wrath is not turned
    back,
    and his hand is still outstretched.

Invasion

²⁶He will give a signal to a far-off nation,
    and whistle to them from the ends of
    the earth;
speedily and promptly will they
    come.
²⁷None of them will stumble with weari-
    ness,
    none will slumber and none will
    sleep.
None will have his waist belt loose,
    nor the thong of his sandal broken.
²⁸Their arrows are sharp,
    and all their bows are bent.
The hoofs of their horses seem like flint,
    and their chariot wheels like the
    hurricane.
²⁹Their roar is that of the lion,
    like the lion's whelps they roar;
They growl and seize the prey,
    they carry it off and none will rescue
    it.
³⁰[They will roar over it, on that day,
    with a roaring like that of the sea.]

II. IMMANUEL PROPHECIES

6 Call of Isaiah. ¹In the year king Uzziah died, I saw the Lord seated on a high and lofty throne, with the train of his garment filling the temple. ²Seraphim were stationed above; each of them had six wings: with two they veiled their

will humble human pride. The sages doubt this and challenge God (and Isaiah) to get on with it. They are pragmatic politicians. Isaiah can only retort by proclaiming the wrath of God.

5:26-30 The Assyrian danger. Isaiah's threat that Yahweh would disrupt the plans of the wise was not totally lacking in practical reason. He does not simply envisage a miracle. God would act through a "far-off nation" (5:26). Isaiah was an astute political observer who saw the menace of Assyria and had no illusions that Judean diplomacy would be able to avert disaster. The complacency of the wise and their self-indulgent lifestyle left them vulnerable to a changing political situation.

6:1-13 The call vision of Isaiah. Isaiah's vision, reported in chapter 6, is usually thought to mark the beginning of a memoir (6:1–8:20) that was recorded in the time of the prophet himself. The vision is dated to an early point in his career (742 B.C.E.). Since it involves the commissioning of the prophet, it is usually regarded as his inaugural vision. Hebrew prophets were thought to receive their message in the heavenly council (compare Jer 23:19,

25

faces, with two they veiled their feet, and with two they hovered aloft.

³"Holy, holy, holy is the Lᴏʀᴅ of hosts!" they cried one to the other. "All the earth is filled with his glory!" ⁴At the sound of that cry, the frame of the door shook and the house was filled with smoke.

⁵Then I said, "Woe is me, I am doomed! For I am a man of unclean lips, living among a people of unclean lips; yet my eyes have seen the King, the Lᴏʀᴅ of

which claims that Jeremiah's opponents have not had this experience). Such visions were not necessarily confined to the beginning of a prophet's career. The closest parallel to Isaiah's vision is attributed to a prophet named Micaiah ben Imlah in 1 Kgs 22, and it is not an inaugural vision.

Isaiah makes the astonishing claim that he has seen the Lord. There is some ambiguity in the Bible as to whether a person can see God. In Exod 33:11 we are told that God used to speak to Moses face-to-face, but also that Moses was only allowed to see God's back, since "my face you cannot see, for no man sees me and still lives" (Exod 33:20; compare Isaiah's fear that he is doomed in 6:5). The prophet Ezekiel sums up his own introductory vision as "the vision of the likeness of the glory of the Lord"—a very circumspect claim (Ezek 1:28). Isaiah, by contrast, is perfectly direct: "I saw the Lord" (6:1). The parallel with the vision of Micaiah ben Imlah in 1 Kgs 22 suggests that there was a prophetic tradition that prophets could indeed see God.

Here it must be said that what a prophet sees in a vision is inevitably conditioned by his preconceptions and by the beliefs of his contemporaries. A prophet in the eighth century ʙ.ᴄ.ᴇ. *could* have a vision of God because it was believed to be possible, and the report would be accepted by a significant number of his contemporaries. God is envisaged as a king because the king was the most powerful and majestic figure in the prophet's experience. (The similarity between the heavenly and earthly courts is more obvious in 1 Kgs 22.) The seraphim in Isaiah's vision are evidently inspired by the cherubim, the hybrid figures in the Jerusalem temple above which Yahweh was supposed to be enthroned.

Isaiah apparently had this vision in the temple, possibly on a cultic occasion when the house was filled with the smoke of incense. Such an experience may not have been unique to prophets. The psalmist speaks of gazing toward God in the temple "to see your power and your glory" (Ps 63:3). It may be that worshipers hoped for such a vision when they attended worship in the temple. In any case, the claim to have seen God lends considerable authority to the prophet's message. If it comes directly from God, it takes precedence over the claims of any human institution.

The cry of the seraphim expresses Isaiah's central affirmation about God: "Holy, holy, holy" (6:3). The significance of God's holiness is shown in the

hosts!" ⁶Then one of the seraphim flew to me, holding an ember which he had taken with tongs from the altar.
⁷He touched my mouth with it. "See," he said, "now that this has touched your lips, your wickedness is removed, your sin purged."
⁸Then I heard the voice of the Lord saying, "Whom shall I send? Who will go for us?" "Here I am;" I said; "send me!" ⁹And he replied: Go and say to this people:

Listen carefully, but you shall not understand!
Look intently, but you shall know nothing!
¹⁰You are to make the heart of this people sluggish,
to dull their ears and close their eyes;
Else their eyes will see, their ears hear, their heart understand,

and they will turn and be healed.

¹¹"How long, O Lord?" I asked. And he replied:

Until the cities are desolate,
without inhabitants,
Houses, without a man,
and the earth is a desolate waste.
¹²Until the LORD removes men far away,
and the land is abandoned more and more.
¹³If there be still a tenth part in it,
then this in turn shall be laid waste;
As with a terebinth or an oak
whose trunk remains when its leaves have fallen.
[Holy offspring is the trunk.]

7 **Birth of Immanuel.** ¹In the days of Ahaz, king of Judah, son of Jotham, son of Uzziah, Rezin, king of Aram, and

prophet's immediate confession of impurity. Isaiah does not recall a specific sin. The impurity is inherent in his human condition and endangers him in the presence of God. The remedy is a drastic one: his lips are purified with a burning coal. An analogous remedy will be prescribed for the whole people.

The prophet's vision is never an end in itself. He is not practicing a life of contemplation. Instead, he is given a message that bears on the political situation in Jerusalem. This message is not to save the people; on the contrary, it ensures their doom by making their hearts sluggish. The prophet's job here is to announce the coming judgment, not to bring about the conversion, at least not directly. We may compare Exod 7:3, where God hardens Pharaoh's heart, thereby setting him up for further destruction.

It would seem, then, that the judgment on Judea cannot be avoided. The question raised by the prophet is not "whether" but "how long?" The answer involves the familiar theme of the remnant. Israel will be like a tree that has been cut down, so that only a stump remains. The editorial gloss, "Holy offspring is the trunk" (6:13), gives the prophecy an upbeat ending. It also is in keeping with the thought of Isaiah that this remnant does indeed have a future. Yet the emphasis in chapter 6 is overwhelmingly negative. The good news of the remnant is overshadowed by the destruction of the majority. The destruction will presumably purify the remnant, as the burning coals purified the prophet's lips.

7:1-25 The prophecy of Immanuel. The opening verse of chapter 7 refers to the campaign of Syria (Aram) and northern Israel (Ephraim) against Judah

Pekah, king of Israel, son of Remaliah, went up to attack Jerusalem, but they were not able to conquer it. ²When word came to the house of David that Aram was encamped in Ephraim, the heart of the king and the heart of the people trembled, as the trees of the forest tremble in the wind.

³Then the LORD said to Isaiah: Go out to meet Ahaz, you and your son Shear-jashub, at the end of the conduit of the upper pool, on the highway of the fuller's field, ⁴and say to him: Take care you remain tranquil and do not fear; let not your courage fail before these two stumps of smoldering brands [the blazing anger of Rezin and the Arameans, and of the son of Remaliah], ⁵because of the mischief that Aram [Ephraim and the son of Remaliah] plots against you, saying, ⁶"Let us go up and tear Judah asunder, make it our own by force, and appoint the son of Tabeel king there."

⁷Thus says the LORD:

This shall not stand, it shall not be!
⁸Damascus is the capital of Aram,
    and Rezin the head of Damascus;
Samaria is the capital of Ephraim,
    and Remaliah's son the head of
        Samaria.
⁹But within sixty years and five,

in the reign of Ahaz. The campaign in question took place between 735 and 733 B.C.E. (see 2 Kgs 16) and is known as the Syro-Ephraimite war. Syria and Israel had already been paying tribute to Assyria since 738 B.C.E. but had now decided to revolt by withholding payment. Judah had refused to join the alliance. As yet Ahaz had no quarrel with Assyria, and in any case hopes of success were remote. Israel and Syria then attempted to overthrow Ahaz and replace him with a king more amenable to their wishes.

The royal ideology of the Davidic dynasty professed a sublime confidence that God would protect his chosen king and city. Recall Ps 46:1-4:

> God is our refuge and our strength,
>   an ever-present help in distress.
> Therefore we fear not, though the earth be shaken
>   and mountains plunge into the depths of the
>   sea . . . .
> The Lord of hosts is with us;
>   our stronghold is the God of Jacob.

Such a profession is easily made when there is no immediate danger. Faced with an actual invasion, however, "the heart of the king and the heart of the people trembled, as the trees of the forest tremble in the wind" (7:2).

At this juncture Isaiah goes to meet Ahaz, who is apparently checking his water supply in anticipation of a siege. Isaiah is accompanied by his son, whose name, Shear-jashub, means "a remnant shall return." His advice to the king is startling. He does not suggest the course that Ahaz would eventually take, to appeal to Assyria for help (2 Kgs 16:7). Instead, he tells him to "remain tranquil and do not fear" (7:4) because the attack will not succeed and the state of northern Israel will soon come to an end. (The refer-

Ephraim shall be crushed, no longer
a nation.
Unless your faith is firm
you shall not be firm!
¹⁰Again the LORD spoke to Ahaz: ¹¹Ask
for a sign from the LORD, your God; let
it be deep as the nether world, or high as
the sky! ¹²But Ahaz answered, "I will not
ask! I will not tempt the LORD! ¹³Then he

said: Listen, O house of David! Is it not
enough for you to weary men, must you
also weary my God? ¹⁴Therefore the Lord
himself will give you this sign: the virgin
shall be with child, and bear a son, and
shall name him Immanuel. ¹⁵He shall be
living on curds and honey by the time he
learns to reject the bad and choose the
good. ¹⁶For before the child learns to re-

ence to "sixty years and five" (7:9) has puzzled commentators. It is too far
away to have immediate relevance for Ahaz, and besides, Israel was effec-
tively terminated in 722 B.C.E. Some scholars suggest that this verse is a gloss
added in 671 B.C.E., when further settlers were brought to Samaria by the
Assyrian king Esar-haddon [see Ezra 4:2]. Others suggest that the original
text read "six years or five" [so the Jerusalem Bible], but there is no textual
evidence for this reading.) The divine commitment to make the Davidic line
"firm" (2 Sam 7:16) is conditional on the faith of the king. (In Hebrew the
words for "firm" and "believe" are derived from the same root.)

The birth of a child. Isaiah then offers Ahaz a sign and proceeds to give
it even when the king refuses to ask for it. The sign is that a young woman
will bear a son who will be "living on curds and honey by the time he learns
to reject the bad and choose the good" (7:15). The mother is called an *almah*
in the Hebrew, that is, a young woman of marriageable age, though not necessarily a virgin. The Greek translation of Isaiah used the word *parthenos*,
which means "virgin" unambiguously, and this translation is cited in Matt
1:22-23 and formed the basis of the traditional Christian interpretation of
this text as a prophecy of the birth of Christ. The Hebrew, however, does
not suggest that the birth in itself was miraculous.

Since the sign was given to Ahaz, we must assume that the young woman
in question was known to him. There are two possible identifications.
The first is the prophet's wife. We know that the prophet gave symbolic names
to his children. The second is the king's wife. The name Immanuel, "God
is with us," could serve as a slogan for the Davidic house. While the prophet
could predict the name of his own child more confidently, a royal child would
be the more effective sign for the king. While either identification is possible, it seems more probable that the woman in question was one of Ahaz's
wives.

The child about to be born will be "living on curds and honey by the
time he learns to reject the bad and choose the good" (7:15). The translation
of this sentence is disputed. It could be that he will live on curds and honey
so that he may learn (so the Vulgate). The age of moral discrimination is

ject the bad and choose the good, the land of those two kings whom you dread shall be deserted.

from Judah. [This means the king of Assyria.] [18]On that day

¹⁷The LORD shall bring upon you and your people and your father's house days worse than any since Ephraim seceded

The LORD shall whistle
    for the fly that is in the farthest
      streams of Egypt,
    and for the bee in the land of Assyria.

usually put at about twenty years. According to this interpretation, Immanuel would be brought up on a diet of curds and honey in order to form his moral discrimination. Some scholars, however, think that the age in question may be much lower—three to five years of age. The lower figure seems more probable in view of 7:16: "For before the child learns to reject the bad and choose the good, the land of those two kings whom you dread shall be deserted." If this sign has any urgency, the interval can be no more than a few years.

The meaning of the sign. The diet of curds and honey is evidently part of the sign and illustrates the ambiguity inherent in this whole passage. The land of Israel was proverbially "a land flowing with milk and honey" (Exod 3:8; 13:5; Num 13:27; Josh 5:6). Such food would appear abundant to nomads from the wilderness; it would surely seem spartan to a king accustomed to live in luxury. The implications of the diet of curds and honey can be seen in 7:21-25: those who remain in the land will have to live on its natural produce, since cultivation will be impossible. Curds and honey will be the only available food. The phrase "On that day" (7:20, 21) suggests that the coming destruction is "the day of the Lord," but it is clear that the instrument of destruction is "the razor hired from across the River" (7:20)—the Assyrians.

Isaiah not only predicts that Syria and Israel will be destroyed but also that Judah will suffer "days worse than any since Ephraim seceded from Judah" (7:17). It would seem from 7:18-20 that the real menace to Judah is seen to come from the Assyrians rather than from the Syro-Ephraimite coalition.

What, then, is signified by the birth of Immanuel? Evidently the name "God is with us" is *not* a promise that God will shelter the king from all harm if only he has faith; rather, it is an ambiguous sign. The presence of God is not always protective. It can also be destructive, as on the "day of the Lord" (see above, chapter 2). Yet it is not entirely destructive. The birth of a child is perhaps the most universal and enduring symbol of hope for the human race. The newborn child does not contribute to military defense or help resolve the dilemmas of the crisis, but he is nonetheless a sign of hope for a new generation. The prophet predicts that he will reach the age of discernment, however bad the times may be. Even if cultivation becomes impossible, people will survive on curds and honey. Moreover, they can recall

¹⁹All of them shall come and settle
in the steep ravines and in the rocky clefts,
on all thornbushes and in all pastures.
²⁰On that day the LORD shall shave with the razor hired from across the River [with the king of Assyria] the head, and the hair between the legs. It shall also shave off the beard.
²¹On that day a man shall keep a heifer or a couple of sheep, ²²and from their abundant yield of milk he shall live on curds; curds and honey shall be the food of all who remain in the land. ²³On that

day every place where there used to be a thousand vines, worth a thousand pieces of silver, shall be turned to briers and thorns. ²⁴Men shall go there with bow and arrows; for all the country shall be briers and thorns. ²⁵For fear of briers and thorns you shall not go upon any mountainside which used to be hoed with the mattock; they shall be grazing land for cattle and shall be trampled upon by sheep.

8 **The Son of Isaiah.** ¹The LORD said to me: Take a large cylinder-seal, and inscribe on it in ordinary letters: "Belong-

a time at the beginning of Israel's history when such a diet was seen as a bountiful gift of God. Isaiah prophesies that the vineyards, worth thousands of pieces of silver, will be overgrown with thorns and briers (see the Song of the Vineyard, Isa 5:6). This would be a loss to the ruling class but not necessarily to the common people. The demise of the vineyards might mark a return to a simpler lifestyle, in which Israel and Judah would be less wealthy, but also less torn by social oppression and less entangled in international politics.

Isaiah's advice to Ahaz, then, is to wait out the crisis, trusting not for miraculous deliverance but for eventual survival. The prophet probably feels that there is no need to fight against Syria and Israel, Assyria will take care of them. Sending for aid to Assyria is probably also unnecessary and would bring Judah directly into subjection. In the meantime Judah might be ravaged and reduced to near wilderness, but life would go on, and the society would be purified in the process.

Ahaz, of course, does not follow Isaiah's advice. He sends gold and silver to the king of Assyria and becomes his vassal. Damascus is destroyed. Samaria survives only because a coup puts a new king on the throne, but even then it survives for a mere decade. The politics of Ahaz seem to work well enough for the present, but Isaiah would surely hold that they do not go to the heart of the matter.

The figure of Immanuel in Isa 7 is not presented as a messianic figure, although he probably was a royal child. Nothing is said of his future reign. Instead, he is a symbol of hope in weakness, of new life in the midst of destruction. When early Christianity read this passage as a prediction of the birth of Jesus, it implied an analogy between the two births. In the Gospels, too, a birth in inauspicious circumstances was nonetheless taken as a sign of the presence of God.

ing to Maher-shalal-hash-baz." ²And I took reliable witnesses, Uriah the priest, and Zechariah, son of Jeberechiah. ³Then I went to the prophetess and she conceived and bore a son. The LORD said to me: Name him Maher-shalal-hash-baz, ⁴for before the child knows how to call his father or mother by name, the wealth of Damascus and the spoil of Samaria shall be carried off by the king of Assyria.

⁵Again the LORD spoke to me:

⁶Because this people has rejected
  the waters of Shiloah that flow gently,
And melts with fear before the loftiness of Rezin and Remaliah's son,
⁷Therefore the LORD raises against them
  the waters of the River, great and mighty
  [the king of Assyria and all his power].
It shall rise above all its channels,

and overflow all its banks;
⁸ It shall pass into Judah, and flood it all throughout:
  up to the neck it shall reach;
It shall spread its wings
  the full width of your land, Immanuel!
⁹Know, O peoples, and be appalled!
  Give ear, all you distant lands!
Arm, but be crushed! Arm, but be crushed!
¹⁰Form a plan, and it shall be thwarted;
  make a resolve, and it shall not be carried out,
  for "With us is God!"

Disciples of Isaiah. ¹¹For thus said the LORD to me, taking hold of me and warning me not to walk in the way of this people:

¹²Call not alliance what this people calls alliance,
  and fear not, nor stand in awe of

8:1-15 Prophecies concerning Assyria. A series of short oracles in chapter 8 throws some light on Isaiah's stance in the crisis of 735–738 B.C.E.

First, the prophet has another child, who becomes a living sign that the Assyrians will plunder Syria and Israel. Unlike Immanuel, this child is explicitly said to be the prophet's son. His relevance to the prophet's prediction, however, is similar: Damascus and Samaria will be destroyed before he begins to talk. The time period is presumably not much less than was implied in the case of Immanuel.

A second short oracle is found in verses 5-10. The people have rejected the waters of Shiloah (a stream in Jerusalem) by not trusting in the divine promises to David and succumbing to fear. The waters of Shiloah flow gently; they are not mighty or threatening. Because the Judeans have not been content with such a passive role, the great river of Assyria, the Euphrates, will flood them. There is pointed irony in this. Ahaz has appealed to Assyria for protection, but the protection of Assyria is overpowering and oppressive in itself. Isaiah is adamant that anyone who resists will be crushed (as indeed they were). The plans of the counselors are in vain, for "With us is God!" (v. 10). Here again the prophet is playing on the name of Immanuel. God is present in the Assyrian onslaught, not with those who resist it.

A third brief oracle in verses 11-15 dismisses political alliances as futile and says that the fear of the people is misplaced—they should fear the Lord.

what they fear.
³But with the LORD of hosts make your
alliance—
for him be your fear and your awe.
⁴Yet he shall be a snare, an obstacle and
a stumbling stone
to both the houses of Israel,
A trap and a snare
to those who dwell in Jerusalem;
⁵And many among them shall stumble
and fall,
broken, snared, and captured.

¹⁶The record is to be folded and the
ealed instruction kept among my dis-
iples. ¹⁷For I will trust in the LORD, who
 hiding his face from the house of Jacob;
'es, I will wait for him. ¹⁸Look at me and
he children whom the Lord has given me:
ve are signs and portents in Israel from
he LORD of hosts who dwells on Mount

Zion. ¹⁹And when they say to you, "Inquire of mediums and fortunetellers (who
chirp and mutter!); should not a people
inquire of their gods, apply to the dead
on behalf of the living?"—²⁰then this
document will furnish its instruction.
That kind of thing they will surely say.

The Prince of Peace. ²³First he degraded the land of Zebulun and the land
of Naphtali; but in the end he has glorified the seaward road, the land west of
the Jordan, the District of the Gentiles.

Anguish has taken wing, dispelled is
darkness:
for there is no gloom where but now
there was distress.

9 ¹The people who walked in darkness
have seen a great light;
Upon those who dwelt in the land of
gloom

he point here is not only that they should fear the Assyrians as God's weapon
ut concerns a basic religious attitude. Isaiah renounces all political intrigue
nd its goal of international power. Yahweh becomes a stumbling block, frus-
ating the designs of the counselors in Jerusalem as well as Samaria. Isaiah
eems to regard political intrigue as sinful in itself. In the context of the As-
yrian crisis, he had, at least, good reason to regard the intrigue of the Israel-
es as ineffectual.

8:16-20 Conclusion of the memoir. This passage gives a rare glimpse
f the formation of a prophetic book. The prophet gives instruction that his
ords be recorded and preserved by his disciples. The memoir (probably
hapters 6–8) is, then, a testimony, a public reminder of the prophet's mes-
age, like the symbolic names of Isaiah's children. It will be available for
onsultation, so that people will not need to resort to mediums and fortune-
ellers (compare the story of Saul in 1 Sam 28). Such signs are necessary when
od is "hiding his face from the house of Jacob" (v. 17). At this juncture
od was most obviously hidden from the northern kingdom, but Isaiah ap-
arently thinks of all Israel as one people, subject to the God who dwells
 Jerusalem on Mount Zion.

8:23–9:6 A new king. The famous prophecy of the birth of a child is
roperly called a "messianic" prophecy because it describes an ideal king
hose reign is still in the future. There is disagreement as to how the oracle
as originally understood. It could refer to the birth of a royal child (com-
are Vergil's famous *Fourth Eclogue*, which was written to celebrate the birth

33

a light has shone.
²You have brought them abundant joy
and great rejoicing,
As they rejoice before you as at the
harvest,
as men make merry when dividing
spoils.

³For the yoke that burdened them,
the pole on their shoulder,
And the rod of their taskmaster
you have smashed, as on the day o
Midian.
⁴For every boot that tramped in battle
every cloak rolled in blood,

of the Roman emperor's son). More probably it was a hymn in honor of the enthronement of a new king (compare Ps 2:7, where the king is told the decree of the Lord: "You are my son, this day I have begotten you"). Apparently the king was adopted as "son of God" when he came to the throne. The king in question in Isa 9 is surely Hezekiah, Ahaz's successor, who became king in either 725 or 715 B.C.E. (the evidence is inconsistent). The earlier date would make better sense here.

Isa 8:23 refers to the dismemberment of northern Israel by the Assyrians in 733–732 B.C.E., when three districts were taken away from Samaria and made Assyrian provinces. It is disputed whether the text should be translated as "he has glorified the seaward road" or "he has oppressed" it. If "glorified" is correct, the prophet is anticipating something that has not yet happened. In any case, chapter 9 announces light for those who live in darkness—new hope for the people of northern Israel oppressed by the Assyrians. The prophet says that God has smashed the oppressor "as on the day of Midian" (a battle described in Judg 7). He probably says this in anticipation, because of his confidence in the new king. The hope for northern Israel is found in the arrival of a new Davidic king in Jerusalem and involves the reunification of Israel.

The titles given to the royal "child," especially "God-Hero" (9:5), suggest that he is more than a human being. There can be no doubt, however, that the prophet Isaiah is thinking of an actual king in Jerusalem in the late eighth century B.C.E. The divine titles are part of the royal ideology. Ps 2:7 declares that the king is the begotten son of God, although this is probably understood as a formula of adoption. Ps 45:7 addresses the king as *elohim,* "god." The king is not considered equal to Yahweh, but he is regarded as a superhuman being.

This king is expected to bring about an era of peace. He will be able to do this because God will give him all the empire governed by David. This, of course, did not come about in the time of Hezekiah, nor has it ever come to pass since then. In the context of Isaiah's message, this is a vision of hope. The glory of the king is still in the future—it is a matter of potential and possibility, not of accomplished fact. The oracle has endured because it formulates a goal of universal peace, which is still desired by humanity.

will be burned as fuel for flames.
⁵For a child is born to us, a son is given
   us;
   upon his shoulder dominion rests.
They name him Wonder-Counselor,
   God-Hero,
   Father-Forever, Prince of Peace.
⁶His dominion is vast
   and forever peaceful,
From David's throne, and over his
   kingdom,
   which he confirms and sustains
By judgment and justice,
   both now and forever.
The zeal of the LORD of hosts will do
   this!

Fall of the Northern Kingdom

⁷The Lord has sent word against Jacob,
   it falls upon Israel;
⁸And all the people know it,
   Ephraim and those who dwell in
      Samaria,
   those who say in arrogance and pride
      of heart,
⁹"Bricks have fallen,
   but we will build with cut stone;
Sycamores are felled,
   but we will replace them with cedars."
¹⁰But the LORD raises up their foes against
   them
   and stirs up their enemies to action:
¹¹Aram on the east and the Philistines on
   the west

devour Israel with open mouth.
For all this, his wrath is not turned back,
   and his hand is still outstretched!
¹²The people do not turn to him who
   struck them,
   nor seek the LORD of hosts.
¹³So the LORD severs from Israel head and
   tail,
   palm branch and reed in one day.
¹⁴[The elder and the noble are the head,
   the prophet who teaches falsehood is
   the tail.]
¹⁵The leaders of this people mislead them
   and those to be led are engulfed.
¹⁶For this reason, the Lord does not spare
   their young men,
   and their orphans and widows he
      does not pity;
They are wholly profaned and sinful,
   and every mouth gives vent to folly.
For all this, his wrath is not turned back,
   his hand is still outstretched!
¹⁷For wickedness burns like fire,
   devouring brier and thorn;
It kindles the forest thickets,
   which go up in columns of smoke.
¹⁸At the wrath of the LORD of hosts the
   land quakes,
   and the people are like fuel for fire;
No man spares his brother,
   each devours the flesh of his neigh-
      bor.
¹⁹Though they hack on the right, they are
   hungry;

Christianity applied this prophecy to the birth of Jesus. In doing so, it disregarded the real political concern of Isaiah for the land of Israel. It picked up instead the fact that these wonderful attributes were attached to a child, to one who has no real power in this world. As in chapter 7 the birth of a child symbolizes the hope of humanity for a brighter future. The prophecy affirms that the key to this future lies in justice and innocence rather than in military might.

9:7-10:4 Judgment on the northern kingdom. We have seen that Isaiah is concerned with the northern kingdom of Israel as well as with his own state of Judah. This series of oracles announces God's judgment on the north. The time in question is not clear; it may have been as early as the Syro-

though they eat on the left, they are
not filled.
²⁰Manasseh devours Ephraim, and
Ephraim Manasseh;
together they turn on Judah.
For all this, his wrath is not turned back,
his hand is still outstretched!

Social Injustice

10 ¹Woe to those who enact unjust
statutes
and who write oppressive decrees,
²Depriving the needy of judgment
and robbing my people's poor of their
rights,
Making widows their plunder,
and orphans their prey!
³What will you do on the day of punishment,
when ruin comes from afar?
To whom will you flee for help?
Where will you leave your wealth,
⁴Lest it sink beneath the captive
or fall beneath the slain?
For all this, his wrath is not turned back,
his hand is still outstretched!

Assyria the Unconscious Instrument of God

⁵Woe to Assyria! My rod in anger,
my staff in wrath.

⁶Against an impious nation I send him,
and against a people under my wrath
I order him
To seize plunder, carry off loot,
and tread them down like the mud of
the streets.
⁷But this is not what he intends,
nor does he have this in mind;
Rather, it is in his heart to destroy,
to make an end of nations not a few.
⁸"Are not my commanders all kings?"
he says,
⁹ "Is not Calno like Carchemish,
Or Hamath like Arpad,
or Samaria like Damascus?
¹⁰Just as my hand reached out to idolatrous kingdoms
that had more images than Jerusalem
and Samaria,
¹¹Just as I treated Samaria and her idols,
shall I not do to Jerusalem and her
graven images?"

¹²[But when the LORD has brought to
an end all his work on Mount Zion and
in Jerusalem,

I will punish the utterance
of the king of Assyria's proud heart,
¹³ and the boastfulness of his haughty
eyes. For he says:]
"By my own power I have done it,

Ephraimite war (see 9:20). The grounds for the judgment are partly arrogance
(9:8), partly the social injustice implied by the pursuit of luxury, and partly
the failure of the Israelites to turn to Yahweh, who, in Isaiah's view, dwells
in Jerusalem (8:18). Since no conversion follows the early setbacks of Israel,
Yahweh's wrath is not turned back, so worse destruction is to come. The
series concludes with a woe-oracle on social injustice that is closely related
to the woe-oracles in chapter 5. Some scholars think that material has been
displaced and that some verses from chapter 5 originally belonged in
chapter 9 (compare the formula in 5:25, which corresponds to 9:11, 16, 20,
and 10:4).

10:5-34 The role of Assyria. Pagan Assyria is the rod with which Yahweh chastises Israel. Yet, Assyria is not itself exempt from judgment, since
its intention is not to serve Yahweh but to wreak destruction. This oracle
is somewhat later than the passages in chapters 7–9. It comes from a time

and by my wisdom, for I am shrewd.
I have moved the boundaries of peoples,
   their treasures I have pillaged,
   and, like a giant, I have put down
      the enthroned.
¹⁴My hand has seized like a nest
   the riches of nations;
As one takes eggs left alone,
   so I took in all the earth;
No one fluttered a wing,
   or opened a mouth, or chirped!"
¹⁵Will the axe boast against him who
      hews with it?
   Will the saw exalt itself above him
      who wields it?
As if a rod could sway him who lifts it,
   or a staff him who is not wood!
¹⁶Therefore the Lord, the LORD of hosts,
   will send among his fat ones leanness,
And instead of his glory there will be
      kindling
   like the kindling of fire.
¹⁷The Light of Israel will become a fire,
   Israel's Holy One a flame,
That burns and consumes his briers
   and his thorns in a single day.
¹⁸His splendid forests and orchards

will be consumed, soul and body;
¹⁹And the remnant of the trees in his
      forest
   will be so few,
Like poles set up for signals,
   that any boy can record them.
²⁰   On that day
The remnant of Israel,
   the survivors of the house of Jacob,
   will no more lean upon him who
      struck them;
But they will lean upon the LORD,
   the Holy One of Israel, in truth.
²¹A remnant will return, the remnant of
      Jacob,
   to the mighty God.
²²For though your people, O Israel,
   were like the sand of the sea,
Only a remnant of them will return;
   their destruction is decreed
   as overwhelming justice demands.
²³Yes, the destruction he has decreed,
the Lord, the GOD of hosts, will carry out
within the whole land. ²⁴Therefore thus
says the Lord, the GOD of hosts: O my
people, who dwell in Zion, do not fear
the Assyrian, though he strikes you with

when Jerusalem rather than Samaria was being threatened, either in 713 B.C.E.
on the occasion of a revolt by Ashdod or in the better-known invasion of
Sennacherib in 701 B.C.E.

The pattern of this oracle is a familiar one in the Bible (see Isa 14; Ezek
27-28). The king of Assyria is guilty of excessive pride, or *hybris*: "By my
own power I have done it, and by my wisdom, for I am shrewd" (v. 13).
In Isaiah's view, human power and wisdom accomplish nothing. Assyria is
an unwitting helper in the plan of God. The prophet's conviction that Assyria would be broken appears to be based on the divine commitment to
Mount Zion. Zion can be struck with a rod (10:24) and so is not protected
from all harm. Yet, the ironic quotation of Assyria's claims in 10:8-11 clearly
implies that Jerusalem is not like Samaria or other cities and cannot be
completely destroyed. So the threatening advance of the Assyrians in verses
28-32 comes close to Jerusalem but stops short of the city. The final assertion of God's majestic power (vv. 33-34) is ambiguous. It is manifested in
the subjection of Judah by the Assyrian advance, but it also casts a shadow
on the Assyrian success and suggests that it too will be cut off.

a rod, and raises his staff against you.
[25]For only a brief moment more, and my
anger shall be over; but them I will destroy in wrath. [26]Then the LORD of hosts
will raise against them a scourge such as
struck Midian at the rock of Oreb; and
he will raise his staff over the sea as he
did against Egypt. [27]On that day,

His burden shall be taken from your
shoulder,
and his yoke shattered from your
neck.

Sennacherib's Invasion

He has come up from the direction of
Rimmon,
[28] he has reached Aiath, passed through
Migron,
at Michmash his supplies are stored.
[29]They cross the ravine:
"We will spend the night at Geba."
Ramah is in terror,
Gibeah of Saul has fled.
[30]Cry and shriek, O daughter of Gallim!
Hearken, Laishah! Answer her,
Anathoth!
[31]Madmenah is in flight,
the inhabitants of Gebim seek refuge.
[32]Even today he will halt at Nob,
he will shake his fist at the mount of
daughter Zion,

the hill of Jerusalem!
[33]Behold, the Lord, the LORD of hosts,
lops off the boughs with terrible violence;
The tall of stature are felled,
and the lofty ones brought low;
[34]The forest thickets are felled with the
axe,
and Lebanon in its splendor falls.

The Rule of Immanuel

11 [1]But a shoot shall sprout from the
stump of Jesse,
and from his roots a bud shall
blossom.
[2]The spirit of the LORD shall rest upon
him:
a spirit of wisdom and of understanding,
A spirit of counsel and of strength,
a spirit of knowledge and of fear of
the LORD.
[3] and his delight shall be the fear of
the LORD.
Not by appearance shall he judge,
nor by hearsay shall he decide,
[4]But he shall judge the poor with justice,
and decide aright for the land's afflicted.
He shall strike the ruthless with the rod
of his mouth,

The passage on the remnant in verses 20-21 is inserted here because of
the occurrence of the word "remnant" in verse 19. The insert shows the typical ambiguity of the remnant: the survivors will be purified and learn to rely
on the Lord, but *only* a remnant will be left. This idea is consistent with
the message of Isaiah throughout his career.

11:1-9 The ideal king. The messianic prophecy in chapter 11 refers more
obviously to a future time than was the case in chapter 9. It is not apparent
that the king in question has even been born. He is described as "a shoot
from the stump of Jesse," that is, from the Davidic line (compare Mic 5:1,
where the lineage is expressed through a reference to Bethlehem, the home
of Jesse). This description does not presuppose that the line had been broken:
"stump" is roughly equivalent to "roots" in the parallel line.

The oracle that follows falls into two parts. Verses 2-5 describe the attributes of the king. The spirit of the Lord will be upon him, and he will

and with the breath of his lips he
shall slay the wicked.
⁵Justice shall be the band around his
waist,
and faithfulness a belt upon his hips.
⁶Then the wolf shall be a guest of the
lamb,
and the leopard shall lie down with
the kid;
The calf and the young lion shall browse
together,
with a little child to guide them.
⁷The cow and the bear shall be neighbors,
together their young shall rest;

the lion shall eat hay like the ox.
⁸The baby shall play by the cobra's
den,
and the child lay his hand on the
adder's lair.
⁹There shall be no harm or ruin on all my
holy mountain;
for the earth shall be filled with
knowledge of the LORD,
as water covers the sea.

Union of Ephraim and Judah

¹⁰ On that day,
The root of Jesse,
set up as a signal for the nations,

do all that a righteous king should do. Verses 6-9 describe a transformation of nature in his reign. This description is quite fantastic, as it concerns a transformation of animal nature that no king could achieve. It is like a return to the garden of Eden. The reference to "all my holy mountain" in verse 9 suggests that the whole earth will then partake of the sanctity of Mount Zion.

It should be obvious that this is a poetic passage, a fantasy of an ideal world rather than a prediction of the future. Such friendship between wolf and lamb has never come about, and there is no reason to think that Isaiah expected it would. Rather, the purpose of this passage is twofold. On the one hand, it is a beautiful picture that comforts the reader in the midst of the turmoil of the Assyrian crisis. On the other hand, it paints a picture of what an ideal world would be like. As such, it presents a challenge for any king. Perhaps Isaiah had come to realize that Hezekiah was not an ideal king, despite the hopes expressed in Isa 9. Indeed, what king could possibly measure up to the ideal presented here? Yet the ideal is important. It reminds us of the imperfections of the present and gives us a goal to work toward, even though we may never fully attain it.

The goal expressed in Isa 11:1-9 is perfect peace, without "harm or ruin"(11:9). In such a world "a little child [will] guide them" (11:6). The motif of the child was prominent in chapter 7 and in the imagery of chapter 9 (but see also 3:12). The child as leader is a contradiction of political and military reality. In Isaiah's view, the power and supposed wisdom of human rulers are of little account. What matters is "the knowledge of the Lord" (v. 9) that goes hand in hand with "the fear of the Lord" (v. 2)—single-minded devotion to justice and abandonment of human pretensions and ambitions.

11:10-16 Reunification of Israel. This oracle of restoration comes from a later time when not only Israel but also Judah had been scattered in exile.

39

The Gentiles shall seek out,
  for his dwelling shall be glorious.
11   On that day,
The Lord shall again take it in hand
  to reclaim the remnant of his people
  that is left from Assyria and Egypt,
Pathros, Ethiopia, and Elam,
  Shinar, Hamath, and the isles of the
  sea.
12He shall raise a signal to the nations
  and gather the outcasts of Israel;
The dispersed of Judah he shall assemble
  from the four corners of the earth.
13The envy of Ephraim shall pass away,
  and the rivalry of Judah be removed;
Ephraim shall not be jealous of Judah,
  and Judah shall not be hostile to
  Ephraim;
14But they shall swoop down on the foot-
  hills
  of the Philistines to the west,
  together they shall plunder the Ked-
  emites;
Edom and Moab shall be their pos-
  sessions,
  and the Ammonites their subjects.
15The Lord shall dry up the tongue of
  the Sea of Egypt,

and wave his hand over the Euphrates
  in his fierce anger
And shatter it into seven streamlets,
  so that it can be crossed in sandals.
16There shall be a highway for the remnant of his people
  that is left from Assyria,
As there was for Israel
  when he came up from the land of
  Egypt.

Song of Thanksgiving

12 ¹   On that day, you will say:
  I give you thanks, O Lord;
  though you have been angry with
  me,
  your anger has abated, and you have
  consoled me.
²God indeed is my savior;
  I am confident and unafraid.
My strength and my courage is the
  Lord,
  and he has been my savior.
³With joy you will draw water
  at the fountain of salvation, ⁴and
  say on that day:
Give thanks to the Lord, acclaim his
  name;

The point of contact with Isaiah's prophecy lies in the opening reference to the root of Jesse. The image of the "signal" or standard for the nations recalls how the nations are said to stream to Mount Zion in chapter 2, but of course the motif of "a light to the nations" is also prominent in Second Isaiah in the exilic period. Here the restoration is presented as a new Exodus (a motif also repeated by Second Isaiah). By contrast, there are no references to the Exodus in those oracles that are ascribed with any confidence to Isaiah himself. The ideal situation envisaged, however, is quite compatible with the hopes of Isaiah. It looks for a reconciliation of Israel and Judah, and their joint sovereignty over the other nations.

12:1-6 A song of thanksgiving. This short hymn of thanksgiving probably concluded an independent booklet of Isaiah's prophecies. The hymn is the work of an editor, despite the use of the characteristically Isaian phrase "the Holy One of Israel" (12:6). The psalmist looks back on hard times but can now praise God, since the crises are past. The judgment oracles of Isaiah are thus put in perspective, for the editor can view these events with hind-

among the nations make known his
deeds,
proclaim how exalted is his name.
⁵Sing praise to the LORD for his glorious
achievement;
let this be known throughout all the
earth.
⁶Shout with exultation, O city of Zion,
for great in your midst
is the Holy One of Israel!

III: ORACLES AGAINST THE PAGAN NATIONS

13 **Babylon.** ¹An oracle concerning Babylon; a vision of Isaiah, son of Amoz.
²Upon the bare mountains set up a
signal;
cry out to them,
Wave for them to enter
the gates of the volunteers.

sight. The reader, too, is encouraged to put the words of Isaiah, bound as they were to specific situations, in a broader, long-term context.

ORACLES AGAINST VARIOUS NATIONS

Isa 13:1–23:8

The oracles in this section are addressed to various foreign nations but include an oracle against Judah and Jerusalem in 22:1-14 and an oracle against a particular official in 22:15-25. Similar collections of oracles against foreign nations are found in Jer 46–51 and Ezek 25–32 (see also Amos 1:3–2:6; Nahum; Obadiah). The number of such prophecies that have survived shows that it was traditional for prophets to predict doom on other nations (and perhaps thereby bring it about—compare the role of the Moabite seer Balaam, who is called on to curse, or prophesy against, Israel in Num 22–24). Usually the prediction of doom on a nation's enemies carries the implication of blessing for the nation itself.

At least some of these oracles come from a time long after Isaiah (for example, the oracles against Babylon in Isa 13–14). Chapter 20 describes an action in Isaiah's own career, and a few passages may be original oracles of the prophet (for example, 14:24-27; 17:1-11). In several other cases there is no clear evidence of origin. We must allow that Isaiah delivered some oracles against foreign nations, that this collection was expanded, and that much of the present collection may not be from the prophet himself.

The oracles against the nations are of historical interest but offer relatively little religious guidance for the modern reader. Here we will comment only on the more notable passages.

13:1-22 The destruction of Babylon. The occasion envisaged by this prophecy is the fall of Babylon to the Medes and Persians, so it was probably composed about 540 B.C.E. Here the destruction of Babylon is "the day of the Lord," a phrase that can be applied to any manifestation of God in judg-

³I have commanded my dedicated sol-
diers,
   I have summoned my warriors,
   eager and bold to carry out my anger.
⁴Listen! the rumble on the mountains:
   that of an immense throng!
Listen! the noise of kingdoms,
   nations assembled!
The LORD of hosts is mustering an army
   for battle.
⁵They come from a far-off country,
   and from the end of the heavens,
The LORD and the instruments of his
   wrath,
   to destroy all the land.
⁶Howl, for the day of the LORD is near;
   as destruction from the Almighty it
   comes.
⁷Therefore all hands fall helpless,
   the bows of the young men fall from
   their hands.
Every man's heart melts ⁸in terror.
   Pangs and sorrows take hold of them,
   like a woman in labor they writhe;
They look aghast at each other,
   their faces aflame.
⁹Lo, the day of the LORD comes,
   cruel, with wrath and burning anger;
To lay waste the land
   and destroy the sinners within it!
¹⁰The stars and constellations of the
   heavens
   send forth no light;
The sun is dark when it rises,
   and the light of the moon does not
   shine.
¹¹Thus I will punish the world for its
   evil
   and the wicked for their guilt.
I will put an end to the pride of the
   arrogant,

the insolence of tyrants I will humble.
¹²I will make mortals more rare than
   pure gold,
   men, than gold of Ophir.
¹³For this I will make the heavens
   tremble
   and the earth shall be shaken from its
   place,
At the wrath of the LORD of hosts
   on the day of his burning anger.
¹⁴Like a hunted gazelle,
   or a flock that no one gathers,
Every man shall turn to his kindred
   and flee to his own land.
¹⁵Everyone who is caught shall be run
   through;
   to a man, they shall fall by the
   sword.
¹⁶Their infants shall be dashed to pieces
   in their sight;
   their houses shall be plundered
   and their wives ravished.
¹⁷I am stirring up against them the Medes,
   who think nothing of silver
   and take no delight in gold.
¹⁸The fruit of the womb they shall not
   spare,
   nor shall they have eyes of pity for
   children.
¹⁹And Babylon, the jewel of kingdoms,
   the glory and pride of the Chaldeans,
Shall be overthrown by God
   like Sodom and like Gomorrah.
²⁰She shall never be inhabited,
   nor dwelt in, from age to age;
The Arab shall not pitch his tent there,
   nor shepherds couch their flocks.
²¹But wildcats shall rest there
   and owls shall fill the houses;
There ostriches shall dwell,
   and satyrs shall dance.

ment. In verses 10-13 the heavens are darkened and the earth shaken. Yet
it is apparent that what the prophet has in mind is a military event, described
in gruesomely realistic terms in verse 16. The cosmic effects are metaphorical. They provide vivid images of the collapse, not of the world at large but
of the world of the Babylonians. This metaphoric use of cosmic imagery plays

²²Desert beasts shall howl in her castles,
   and jackals in her luxurious palaces.
   Her time is near at hand
   and her days shall not be prolonged.

14 The King of Babylon.

¹When the Lord has pity on Jacob and again chooses Israel and settles them on their own soil, the aliens will join them and be counted with the house of Jacob. ²The house of Israel will take them and bring them along to its place, and possess them as male and female slaves on the Lord's soil, making captives of its captors and ruling over its oppressors. ³On the day the Lord relieves you of sorrow and unrest and the hard service in which you have been enslaved, ⁴you will take up this taunt-song against the king of Babylon:

How the oppressor has reached his
      end!
   how the turmoil is stilled!
⁵The Lord has broken the rod of the
      wicked,
   the staff of the tyrants
⁶That struck the peoples in wrath relent-
      less blows;
   That beat down the nations in anger,
   with oppression unchecked.
⁷The whole earth rests peacefully,
   song breaks forth;
⁸The very cypresses rejoice over you,
   and the cedars of Lebanon:
   "Now that you are laid to rest,

   there will be none to cut us down."
⁹The nether world below is all astir
   preparing for your coming;
   It awakens the shades to greet you,
   all the leaders of the earth;
   It has the kings of all nations
   rise from their thrones.
¹⁰All of them speak out
   and say to you,
   "You too have become weak like us,
   you are the same as we.
¹¹Down to the nether world your pomp
      is brought,
   the music of your harps.
   The couch beneath you is the maggot,
   your covering, the worm."
¹²How have you fallen from the heavens,
   O morning star, son of the dawn!
   How are you cut down to the ground,
   you who mowed down the nations!
¹³You said in your heart:
   "I will scale the heavens;
   Above the stars of God
   I will set up my throne;
   I will take my seat on the Mount of
      Assembly,
   in the recesses of the North.
¹⁴I will ascend above the tops of the
      clouds;
   I will be like the Most High!"
¹⁵Yet down to the nether world you go
   to the recesses of the pit!
¹⁶When they see you they will stare,

an important part in other sections of the book and in later apocalyptic literature.

14:1-22 The king of Babylon. The taunt-song against the king of Babylon is famous for its comparison with "Lucifer, Son of Dawn." The comparison is drawn from an ancient Canaanite myth, where Attar, the Daystar, tries to occupy the throne of Baal. The pattern of the story is a very popular one in the Bible. Whoever tries to rise too high will be cast down lowest of all. In a sense this was already the pattern of the story of Adam and Eve, who were cast out of the garden because they wanted to be like God (see Isa 14:14). The same pattern is found in Ezek 27 and 28. By contrast, the pattern is inverted in the case of Jesus, according to Phil 2. Because he did not deem equality with God something to be grasped at, he received a name

43

pondering over you:
"Is this the man who made the earth
    tremble,
    and kingdoms quake?
¹⁷Who made the world a desert,
    razed its cities,
    and gave his captives no release?
¹⁸All the kings of the nations lie in glory,
    each in his own tomb;
¹⁹But you are cast forth without burial,
    loathsome and corrupt,
Clothed as those slain at sword-point,
    a trampled corpse.
Going down to the pavement of the
    pit,
²⁰   you will never be one with them in
    the grave."
For you have ruined your land,
    you have slain your people!
Let him not be named forever,
    that scion of an evil race!
²¹Make ready to slaughter his sons
    for the guilt of their fathers;
Lest they rise and possess the earth,

and fill the breadth of the world with
    tyrants.
²²I will rise up against them, says the
LORD of hosts, and cut off from Babylon
name and remnant, progeny and offspring, says the LORD. ²³I will make it a
haunt of hoot owls and a marshland; I
will sweep it with the broom of destruction, says the LORD of hosts.

Assyria

²⁴   The LORD of hosts has sworn:
As I have resolved,
    so shall it be;
As I have proposed,
    so shall it stand:
²⁵I will break the Assyrian in my land
    and trample him on my mountains;
²¹He shall pass through it hard-pressed
    and hungry,
    and in his hunger he shall become
    enraged,
    and curse his king and his gods.
He shall look upward,

above every other name. The model of Lucifer can obviously be applied to many figures in history besides the king of Babylon. (Lucifer in this context is simply the Daystar, a heavenly being, but is not identified as Satan. This model, however, played a part in the popular legend of the fall of Satan from heaven, which was developed by John Milton in *Paradise Lost*.)

One other aspect of these chapters should be noted. The prophet evidently delights in the overthrow of Babylon. There is a certain amount of vengeful-ness here and considerable resentment toward the overlord—an emotion that superpowers often arouse in less powerful people. This aspect of the prophe-cies may not be to everyone's taste, although anyone engaged in a struggle for liberation will surely resonate with it. It may not be the ideal attitude toward our enemies, but it is at least realistic. Few people get through life without such sentiments. It is better to express them than to deny them hypocritically. The taunts against Babylon are echoed in the New Testament Book of Revelation (chs. 17–18) to vent the feelings of some early Christians against Rome.

14:24-27 The destruction of Assyria. This brief oracle appears out of context here. It suggests that God will allow the Assyrian to invade Israel and will break him there. It raises the question of how Isaiah envisaged God's

but there shall be strict darkness
    without any dawn;
22He shall gaze at the earth,
    but there shall be distress and dark-
        ness,
    with the light blacked out by its
        clouds.
(25)Then his yoke shall be removed from
    them,
  and his burden from their shoulder.
26This is the plan proposed for the whole
    earth,
    and this the hand outstretched over
      all nations.
27The Lord of hosts has planned;
    who can thwart him?
His hand is stretched out;
    who can turn it back?

Philistia. 28In the year that King Ahaz
died, there came this oracle:

29Rejoice not, O Philistia, not a man of
    you,
    that the rod which smote you is
      broken;
For out of the serpent's root shall come
    an adder,
    its fruit shall be a flying saraph.
30In my pastures the poor shall eat,
    and the needy lie down in safety;
But I will kill your root with famine
    that shall slay even your remnant.
31Howl, O gate; cry out, O city!
    Philistia, all of you melts away!
For there comes a smoke from the
    north,
    without a straggler in the ranks.
32What will one answer the messengers of
    the nation?
    "The Lord has established Zion,
  and in her the afflicted of his people
    find refuge."

Moab

15 ¹ Oracle on Moab:
Laid waste in a night,
Ar of Moab is destroyed;

Laid waste in a night,
    Kir of Moab is destroyed.
2Up goes daughter Dibon
    to the high places to weep;
Over Nebo and over Medeba
    Moab wails.
Every head is shaved,
    every beard sheared off.
3In the streets they wear sackcloth,
    lamenting and weeping;
On rooftops and in the squares
    everyone wails.
4Heshbon and Elealeh cry out,
    they are heard as far as Jahaz.
At this the loins of Moab tremble,
    his soul quivers within him;
5The heart of Moab cries out,
    his fugitives reach Zoar
    [Eglath-shelishiyah].
The ascent of Luhith
    they climb weeping;
On the way to Horonaim
    they utter rending cries.
6The waters of Nimrim
    have become a waste;
The grass is withered,
    new growth is gone,
    nothing is green.
7So now whatever they have acquired or
    stored away
    they carry across the Gorge of the
      Poplars,
8For the cry has gone round
    the land of Moab;
As far as Eglaim the wailing, and to
    Beer-elim, the wail.
9The waters of Dimon were filled with
    blood,
    but I will bring still more upon
    Dimon:
Lions for those who are fleeing from
    Moab
    and for those who remain in the land!

16 ¹Send them forth, hugging the
earth like reptiles,
    from Sela across the desert,

overall plan for Israel and Assyria. We will return to this question when we
discuss chapter 29 below.

to the mount of daughter Zion.
²Like flushed birds,
  like startled nestlings,
Are the daughters of Moab
  at the fords of the Arnon.
³Offer counsel, take their part:
  at high noon let your shadow be like
    the night,
To hide the outcasts,
  to conceal the fugitives.
⁴Let the outcasts of Moab live with you,
  be their shelter from the destroyer.
When the struggle is ended, the ruin
  complete,
  and they have done with trampling
    the land,
⁵A throne shall be set up in mercy,
  and on it shall sit in fidelity
  [in David's tent]
A judge upholding right
  and prompt to do justice.
⁶We have heard of the pride of Moab,
  how very proud he is,
With his haughty, arrogant insolence
  that his empty words do not match.
⁷Therefore Moab wails for Moab,
  everywhere they wail;
For the raisin cakes of Kir-hareseth
  they sigh, stricken with grief.
⁸The terraced slopes of Heshbon
  languish,
  the vines of Sibmah,
Whose clusters overpowered
  the lords of nations,
While they reached as far as Jazer
  and scattered over the desert,
And whose branches spread forth
  and extended over the sea.
⁹Therefore I weep with Jazer
  for the vines of Sibmah;
I water you with tears,
  Heshbon and Elealeh;
For on your summer fruits and harvests
  the battle cry has fallen.
¹⁰From the orchards are taken away

joy and gladness,
In the vineyards there is no singing,
  no shout of joy;
In the wine presses no one treads grapes,
  the vintage shout is stilled.
¹¹Therefore for Moab
  my breast moans like a lyre,
  and my heart for Kir-hareseth.
¹²When Moab grows weary on the high
    places,
  he shall enter his sanctuary to pray,
  but it shall avail him nothing.
¹³This is the word the LORD spoke
against Moab in times past. ¹⁴But now the
LORD has spoken: In three years, like
those of a hireling, the glory of Moab
shall be degraded despite all its great mul-
titude; there shall be a remnant, very
small and weak.

Damascus

17 ¹ Oracle on Damascus:
  Lo, Damascus shall cease to be a
    city
  and become a ruin;
²Her cities shall be forever abandoned,
  given over to flocks to lie in undis-
    turbed.
³The fortress shall be lost to Ephraim
  and the kingdom to Damascus;
The remnant of Aram shall have the
    same glory
  as the Israelites,
  says the LORD of hosts.
⁴ On that day
The glory of Jacob shall fade,
  and his full body grow thin,
⁵Like the reaper's mere armful of stalks
  when he gathers the standing grain;
Or as when one gleans the ears
  in the Valley of Rephaim.
⁶Only a scattering of grapes shall be
    left!
  As when an olive tree has been
    beaten,

17:1-11 Oracle against Syria and northern Israel. This passage is an
authentic oracle of Isaiah from the time of the Syro-Ephraimite war. The

Two or three olives remain at the very
top,
four or five on its fruitful branches,
says the LORD, the God of Israel.
⁷On that day man shall look to his
maker,
his eyes turned toward the Holy One
of Israel.
⁸He shall not look to the altars, his handiwork,
nor shall he regard what his fingers
have made:
the sacred poles or the incense
stands.
⁹On that day his strong cities shall be
like those abandoned by the Hivites
and Amorites
When faced with the children of Israel:
they shall be laid waste.
¹⁰For you have forgotten God, your
savior,
and remembered not the Rock, your
strength.
Therefore, though you plant your pagan
plants
and set out your foreign vine slips,
¹¹Though you make them grow the day
you plant them
and make your sprouts blossom on
the next morning.
The harvest shall disappear on the day

of the grievous blow,
the incurable blight.
¹²Ah! the roaring of many peoples
that roar like the roar of the seas!
The surging of nations
that surge like the surging of mighty
waves!
¹³But God shall rebuke them,
and they shall flee far away;
Windswept, like chaff on the mountains,
like tumbleweed in a storm.
¹⁴In the evening, they spread terror,
before morning, they are gone!
Such is the portion of those who despoil
us,
the lot of those who plunder us.

Ethiopia

18 ¹Ah, land of buzzing insects,
beyond the rivers of Ethiopia,
²Sending ambassadors by sea,
in papyrus boats on the waters!
Go, swift messengers,
to a nation tall and bronzed,
To a people dreaded near and far,
a nation strong and conquering,
whose land is washed by rivers.
³All you who inhabit the world,
who dwell on earth,

prediction is that Syria and northern Israel will be brought low, so that they will come to respect the Holy One of Israel.

17:12-14 The turbulent nations. Chapter 17 concludes with a general statement on the nations, which has many parallels in the psalms (for example, Psalms 2, 48). The viewpoint in these verses is that of the Jerusalem cult, which Isaiah shared only with qualifications. The presupposition is that Yahweh and the nations are in opposition. The conflict is expressed through a metaphor drawn from Canaanite myth. The Canaanites had a story in which the god Baal, the god of fertility, is challenged by the unruly figure of Yamm (the Sea) but proceeds to trounce him with two clubs. Here the nations are like Yamm, turbulent rebels, but the same fate will befall them. God's ability to rebuke the sea is given as testimony to the divine power in the Old Testament (Nah 1:4; Ps 106:9). The same motif is used to show the divinity of Jesus in the New Testament (Matt 8:23-27 and parallels).

When the signal is raised on the mountain, look!
When the trumpet blows, listen!
⁴For thus says the LORD to me:
I will quietly look on from where I dwell,
Like the glowing heat of sunshine,
like a cloud of dew at harvest time.
⁵Before the vintage, when the flowering is ended,
and the blooms are succeeded by ripening grapes,
Then comes the cutting of branches with pruning hooks
and the discarding of the lopped-off shoots.
⁶They shall all be left to the mountain birds of prey,
and to the beasts in the land;
The birds of prey shall summer on them
and on them all the beasts of the earth shall winter.
⁷Then will gifts be brought to the LORD of hosts from a people tall and bronzed, from a people dreaded near and far, a nation strong and conquering, whose land is washed by rivers—to Mount Zion where dwells the name of the LORD of hosts.

Egypt

19¹ Oracle on Egypt:
See, the LORD is riding on a swift cloud
on his way to Egypt;
The idols of Egypt tremble before him,
the hearts of the Egyptians melt with in them.
²I will rouse Egypt against Egypt:
brother will war against brother,
Neighbor against neighbor,
city against city, kingdom against kingdom.
³The courage of the Egyptians ebbs away within them,
and I will bring to nought their counsel;
They shall consult idols and charmers, ghosts and spirits.
⁴I will deliver Egypt
into the power of a cruel master,
A harsh king who shall rule over them,
says the Lord, the LORD of hosts.
⁵The waters shall be drained from the sea,
the river shall shrivel and dry up;
⁶Its streams shall become foul,
and the canals of Egypt shall dwindle and dry up.
Reeds and rushes shall wither away,
⁷ and bulrushes on the bank of the Nile;
All the sown land along the Nile
shall dry up and blow away, and be no more.
⁸The fishermen shall mourn and lament,
all who cast hook in the Nile;
Those who spread their nets in the water shall pine away.
⁹The linen-workers shall be disappointed,
the combers and weavers shall turn pale;
¹⁰The spinners shall be crushed,
all the hired laborers shall be despondent.
¹¹Utter fools are the princes of Zoan!
the wisest of Pharaoh's advisors give stupid counsel.
How can you say to Pharaoh,
"I am a disciple of wise men, of ancient kings"?
¹²Where then are your wise men?
Let them tell you and make known
What the LORD of hosts has planned against Egypt.
¹³The princes of Zoan have become fools,
the princes of Memphis have been deceived.

19:1-15 Oracles against Egypt. It is uncertain whether any of these oracles actually come from Isaiah. We should note at least that the taunts against the sages of Egypt in verses 11-15 recall Isaiah's quarrel with the sages of

The chiefs of her tribes
    have led Egypt astray.
The LORD has prepared among them
    a spirit of dizziness,
And they have made Egypt stagger in
    whatever she does,
    as a drunkard staggers in his vomit.
⁵Egypt shall have no work to do
    for head or tail, palm branch or reed.

¹⁶On that day the Egyptians shall be like women, trembling with fear, because of the LORD of hosts shaking his fist at them. ¹⁷And the land of Judah shall be a terror to the Egyptians. Every time they remember Judah, they shall stand in dread because of the plan which the LORD of hosts has in mind for them.

¹⁸On that day there shall be five cities in the land of Egypt speaking the language of Canaan and swearing by the LORD of hosts; one shall be called "City of the Sun."

¹⁹On that day there shall be an altar to the LORD in the land of Egypt, and a sacred pillar to the LORD near the boundary. ²⁰It shall be a sign and a witness to the LORD of hosts in the land of Egypt, when they cry out to the LORD against their oppressors, and he sends them a savior to defend and deliver them. ²¹The LORD shall make himself known to Egypt, and the Egyptians shall know the LORD in that day; they shall offer sacrifices and oblations, and fulfill the vows they make to the LORD. ²²Although the LORD shall smite Egypt severely, he shall heal them; they shall turn to the LORD and he shall be won over and heal them.

²³On that day there shall be a highway from Egypt to Assyria; the Assyrians shall enter Egypt, and the Egyptians enter Assyria, and Egypt shall serve Assyria.

²⁴On that day Israel shall be a third party with Egypt and Assyria, a blessing in the midst of the land, ²⁵when the LORD of hosts blesses it: "Blessed be my people Egypt, and the work of my hands Assyria, and my inheritance, Israel."

20 Captivity of Egypt and Ethiopia. ¹In the year the general sent by Sargon, king of Assyria, fought against

Jerusalem (5:18-25). Isaiah's interest in Egypt comes from the fact that Egypt is a potential ally, and Judah might be tempted to rely on Egyptian aid.

19:16-24 The future of Egypt. The short oracles with which the chapter concludes are less likely to come from Isaiah. They fantasize how in the future Egypt will fear Judah and come to worship the Lord. Here we must recognize the desire of the powerless little state to get the upper hand over its powerful neighbor. We know that there were Jewish temples in Egypt at Elephantine (about 400 B.C.E.) and at Leontopolis (about 150 B.C.E.), although this was contrary to the law in Deuteronomy. It is unlikely that the passage in Isaiah had either of these in mind. It is simply indulging in a fantasy about the conversion of the Gentiles. Verses 23-24 add another fantasy—that one day Israel will rank as a third world power with Egypt and Assyria. This fantasy was never realized (at least until modern times!). It is strangely in contradiction to the ideals of Isaiah as we have seen them in chapters 2–11, where he held that Judah would be better off to renounce all ambition in the international arena.

20:1-6 A naked prophet. Symbolic actions were a favorite device of the prophets to dramatize their message. Hosea married a harlot. Ezekiel per-

Ashdod and captured it, ²the LORD gave a warning through Isaiah, the son of Amoz: Go and take off the sackcloth from your waist, and remove the sandals from your feet. This he did, walking naked and barefoot. ³Then the LORD said: Just as my servant Isaiah has gone naked and barefoot for three years as a sign and portent against Egypt and Ethiopia, ⁴so shall the king of Assyria lead away captives from Egypt, and exiles from Ethiopia, young and old, naked and barefoot, with buttocks uncovered [the shame of Egypt]. ⁵They shall be dismayed and ashamed because of Ethiopia, their hope, and because of Egypt, their boast. ⁶The inhabitants of this coastland shall say on that day, "Look at our hope! We have fled here for help and deliverance from the king of Assyria; where can we flee now?"

Fall of Babylon

21 ¹ Oracle on the wastelands by the sea:
Like whirlwinds sweeping in waves
    through the Negeb,
there comes from the desert,
from the fearful land,

²A cruel sight, revealed to me:
    the traitor betrays,
    the despoiler spoils.
"Go up, Elam; besiege, O Media;
    I will put an end to all groaning!"
³Therefore my loins are filled with anguish,
    pangs have seized me like those of a
        woman in labor;
I am too bewildered to hear,
    too dismayed to look.
⁴My mind reels,
    shuddering assails me;
My yearning for twilight
    has turned into dread.
⁵They set the table,
    spread out the rugs;
    they eat, they drink.
Rise up, O princes,
    oil the shield!
⁶For thus says my LORD to me:
    Go, station a watchman,
    let him tell what he sees.
⁷If he sees a chariot,
    a pair of horses,
Someone riding an ass,
    someone riding a camel,
Then let him pay heed,
    very close heed.

formed numerous strange acts, including the use of dung to cook his food (Ezek 4). Here we find that Isaiah went naked for three years at the time of the rebellion of Ashdod (713 B.C.E.). This was a sign that Egypt and Ethiopia would fall to Assyria, and the captives would be led away naked.

The symbolic action is a kind of street theatre. It grabs the attention and presents the passerby with a visual image more powerful than any speech. How the people react is, of course, up to them. First they must find out what the sign means, then decide what to do about it. In this case the sign is not performed for the benefit of Egyptians or Ethiopians; rather, it is meant to show the people of Judah and the coastland the folly of relying on Egyptian aid. Egypt was not in fact conquered, but it did not protect the rebels either. Isaiah's warning was justified.

21:1-10 The fall of Babylon. Yet another oracle on the fall of Babylon in the sixth century is inserted here. Two points should be noted. The phrase "Fallen, fallen is Babylon," (21:9) is picked up and applied to Rome in Rev 18:2. The significance of this message for the Jews is underlined in verse 10.

⁸ Then the watchman cried,
"On the watchtower, O my LORD,
I stand constantly by day;
And I stay at my post
through all the watches of the night.
⁹Here he comes now:
a single chariot,
a pair of horses;
He calls out and says,
'Fallen, fallen is Babylon,
And all the images of her gods
are smashed to the ground.' "
¹⁰O my people who have been threshed,
beaten on my threshing floor!
What I have heard
from the LORD of hosts,
The God of Israel,
I have announced to you.

Edom

¹¹ Oracle on Edom:
They call to me from Seir,
"Watchman, how much longer the
night?
Watchman, how much longer the
night?"
¹² The watchman replies,
"Morning has come, and again night.
If you will ask, ask; come back
again."

Arabia

¹³ Oracle on Arabia:
In the thicket in the nomad country
spend the night,
O caravans of Dedanites.
¹⁴Meet the thirsty, bring them water;
you who dwell in the land of Tema,
greet the fugitives with bread.

¹⁵They flee from the sword,
from the whetted sword;
From the taut bow,
from the fury of battle.
¹⁶For thus says the Lord to me: In another year, like those of a hireling, all the glory of Kedar shall come to an end. ¹⁷Few of Kedar's stalwart archers shall remain, for the LORD, the God of Israel, has spoken.

Jerusalem

22 ¹ Oracle of the Valley of Vision:
What is the matter with you now, that
you have gone up,
all of you, to the housetops,
²O city full of noise and chaos,
O wanton town!
Your slain are not slain with the sword,
nor killed in battle.
³All your leaders fled away together,
fled afar off;
All who were in you were captured
together,
captured without the use of a bow.
⁴At this I say: Turn away from me,
let me weep bitterly;
Do not try to comfort me
for the ruin of the daughter of my
people.
⁵It is a day of panic, rout and confusion,
from the Lord, the GOD of hosts,
in the Valley of Vision.
Walls crash;
they cry for help to the mountains.
⁶Elam takes up the quivers,
Aram mounts the horses,
and Kir uncovers the shields.
⁷Your choice valleys are filled with chariots,

Judah has been threshed and winnowed by Babylon—she can hardly fail to delight in the fall of the oppressor.

22:1-14 The fall of Jerusalem. This lone oracle against Jerusalem is included in the oracles against the nations, perhaps to make the point that Judah, too, is subject to judgment (compare the treatment of Israel in Amos 1–2). Much of this oracle presupposes the actual fall of Jerusalem to the Babylonians in 587–586 B.C.E. (so 22:4-11). Some scholars, however, recognize

and horses are posted at the gates,
8 and shelter over Judah is removed.

On that day you looked to the weapons in the House of the Forest; ⁹you saw that the breaches in the City of David were many; you collected the water of the lower pool. ¹⁰You numbered the houses of Jerusalem, tearing some down to strengthen the wall; ¹¹you made a reservoir between the two walls for the water of the old pool. But you did not look to the city's Maker, nor did you consider him who built it long ago.
¹²On that day the Lord,
the GOD of hosts, called on you
To weep and mourn,
to shave your head and put on sackcloth.
¹³But look! you feast and celebrate,
you slaughter oxen and butcher sheep,
You eat meat and drink wine:
"Eat and drink, for tomorrow we die!"
¹⁴This reaches the ears of the LORD of hosts—
You shall not be pardoned this wickedness till you die,
says the Lord, the GOD of hosts.

Shebna and Eliakim

¹⁵Thus says the Lord, the GOD of hosts
Up, go to that official,
Shebna, master of the palace,
¹⁶Who has hewn for himself a sepulchre on a height
and carved his tomb in the rock:
"What are you doing here, and what people have you here,
that here you have hewn for yourself a tomb?"
¹⁷The LORD shall hurl you down headlong, mortal man!
He shall grip you firmly
¹⁸And roll you up and toss you like a ball into an open land
To perish there, you and the chariots you glory in,
you disgrace to your master's house
¹⁹I will thrust you from your office
and pull you down from your station
²⁰On that day I will summon my servant Eliakim, son of Hilkiah;
²¹I will clothe him with your robe,
and gird him with your sash,
and give over to him your authority
He shall be a father to the inhabitants of Jerusalem,
and to the house of Judah.

an oracle of Isaiah in verses 1-3 and 12-14, which presuppose that the city did not fall. This oracle may have been delivered on the occasion of Sennacherib's campaign against Jerusalem, which we will examine below in Isa 36–39.

In verses 1-3a the prophet chides the people of Jerusalem for their panic and lack of trust. Then in verses 12-14 he rebukes them because they turned too easily to celebrating instead of taking their narrow escape as an occasion for repentance. The slogan attributed to the revelers, "Eat and drink, for tomorrow we die!" (22:13), is often quoted (see Isa 56:12; Wis 2:6; 1 Cor 15:32). The force of the prophet's criticism may be that the people in Jerusalem did not show enough concern for the sufferings of their fellow Judeans and did not take the lesson of the folly of rebellion to heart.

22:15-25 Rivals at court. The two officials who are the subjects of verses 15-25 are also mentioned in Isa 36 and 2 Kgs 18, where Eliakim is called "master of the palace." The oracle cited here may have been setting a seal

²²I will place the key of the House of
David on his shoulder;
when he opens, no one shall shut,
when he shuts, no one shall open.
²³I will fix him like a peg in a sure spot,
to be a place of honor for his family;
²⁴On him shall hang all the glory of his
family:
descendants of offspring,
all the little dishes, from bowls to
jugs.

²⁵On that day, says the LORD of hosts,
the peg fixed in a sure spot shall give way,
break off and fall, and the weight that
hung on it shall be done away with; for
the LORD has spoken.

Tyre and Sidon

23 ¹ Oracle on Tyre:
Wail, O ships of Tarshish,
for your port is destroyed;
From the land of the Kittim
the news reaches them.
²Silence! you who dwell on the coast,
you merchants of Sidon,
Whose messengers crossed the sea
³ over the deep waters.
The grain of Shihor, the harvest of
the Nile, was her revenue,
and she the merchant among nations.
⁴Shame, O Sidon, fortress on the sea, for
the sea has spoken:
"I have not been in labor, nor given
birth,
nor raised young men,
nor reared virgins."
⁵When it is heard in Egypt
they shall be in anguish at the news of
Tyre.
⁶Pass over to Tarshish, wailing,
you who dwell on the coast!
⁷Is this your wanton city,

whose origin is from of old,
Whose feet have taken her
to dwell in distant lands?
⁸Who has planned such a thing
against Tyre, the bestower of crowns,
Whose merchants are princes,
whose traders are the earth's honored
men?
⁹The LORD of hosts has planned it,
to disgrace all pride of majesty,
to degrade all the earth's honored
men.
¹⁰Cross to your own land,
O ship of Tarshish;
the harbor is no more.
¹¹His hand he stretches out over the sea,
he shakes kingdoms;
The LORD has ordered the destruction
of Canaan's strongholds.
¹²You shall exult no more, he says,
you who are now oppressed, virgin
daughter Sidon.
Arise, pass over to the Kittim, even
there you shall find no rest.
¹³[This people is the land of the Chaldeans, not Assyria.]
She whom the impious founded,
setting up towers for her,
Has had her castles destroyed,
and has been turned into a ruin.
¹⁴Lament, O ships of Tarshish,
for your haven is destroyed.
¹⁵On that day, Tyre shall be forgotten
for seventy years. With the days of
another king, at the end of seventy years,
it shall be for Tyre as in the song about
the harlot:
¹⁶Take a harp, go about the city,
O forgotten harlot;
Pluck the strings skillfully, sing many
songs,
that they may remember you.

of divine approval on a reorganization of the royal cabinet. The wrath of
the prophet is aroused by the luxury of Shebna, especially the tomb he has
prepared for himself. The prophet sees this as an attempt to control his fate,
which will be frustrated by God. He also objects to Shebna's delight in chariots. It is interesting to see the prophet engaging in day-to-day politics and

¹⁷At the end of the seventy years the LORD shall visit Tyre. She shall return to her hire and deal with all the world's kingdoms on the face of the earth. ¹⁸But her merchandise and her hire shall be sacred to the LORD. It shall not be stored up or laid away, but from her merchandise those who dwell before the LORD shall eat their fill and clothe themselves in choice attire.

IV: APOCALYPSE OF ISAIAH
Devastation of the World:
A Remnant Saved

24 ¹Lo, the LORD empties the land and lays it waste;
he turns it upside down,
scattering its inhabitants:
²Layman and priest alike,
servant and master,
The maid as her mistress,
the buyer as the seller,
The lender as the borrower,
the creditor as the debtor.
³The earth is utterly laid waste, utterly stripped,
for the LORD has decreed this thing.
⁴The earth mourns and fades,
the world languishes and fades;
both heaven and earth languish.
⁵The earth is polluted because of its inhabitants,
who have transgressed laws, violated statutes,
broken the ancient covenant.
⁶Therefore a curse devours the earth,
and its inhabitants pay for their guilt;
Therefore they who dwell on earth turn pale,
and a few men are left.

endorsing one official against another. Such participation in political life is necessary for anyone who seriously wants to influence public policy.

THE APOCALYPSE OF ISAIAH

Isa 24:1–27:13

These chapters stand out from their context, as they are much less specific than the oracles against foreign nations which precede them. They are loosely structured and were not necessarily composed as a coherent unit. Attempts to tie them to a specific historical setting have usually focused on allusions to the destruction of a city (24:10-12; 25:1-5; 26:5; 27:10-11). The city in question has been identified with a whole spectrum of cities from Babylon in the sixth century B.C.E. to Samaria in the second. It is not certain, however, that all references are to the same city or that all passages envisage a specific city at all. If the references are to a single city, the most likely referent is Babylon, but the lack of specific detail makes these chapters into a general description of a desolate world and the hope for definitive salvation through the power of God.

24:1-20 The desolation of the earth. This passage reads like a ritual mourning for the land. We may compare Joel 1-2, but there the occasion is quite specific—it is a plague of locusts. In Isa 24 the occasion is not clear

⁷The wine mourns, the vine languishes,
all the merry-hearted groan.
⁸Stilled are the cheerful timbrels,
ended the shouts of the jubilant,
stilled is the cheerful harp.
⁹They cannot sing and drink wine;
strong drink is bitter to those who
partake of it.
⁰Broken down is the city of chaos,
shut against entry, every house.
¹In the streets they cry out for lack of
wine;
all joy has disappeared
and cheer has left the land.
²In the city nothing remains but ruin;
its gates are battered and desolate.

¹³Thus it is within the land,
and among the peoples,
As with an olive tree after it is beaten,
as with a gleaning when the vintage is
done.
¹⁴These lift up thir voice in acclaim;
from the sea they proclaim the majesty of the Lord:
¹⁵"For this, in the coastlands,
give glory to the Lord!
In the coastlands of the sea,
to the name of the Lord, the God of
Israel!"
¹⁶From the end of the earth we hear songs:
"Splendor to the Just One!"
But I said, "I am wasted, wasted away.

at all. It may have been a severe drought or some unspecified historical crisis. Some scholars identify the "city of chaos" in verse 10 as a particular city
(for example, Babylon, when it was destroyed by Xerxes of Persia in
482 B.C.E.), but it may also be read as a more general reference. Just as the
whole land is turned upside down, cities too are reduced to chaos. Special
attention is paid to the lack of wine, which dampens festivity (v. 11). The
disorders extend also to social relations. Distinctions in status break down.
Servant and master are on equal footing. The prophet is developing themes
which we have seen already in Isa 2–3 and which were associated with the
"day of the Lord" (see also Joel 1–2). The destruction of the earth and the
breakdown of social order are seen as manifestations of the majesty of God
and correctives to human pride. Hence the surprising call to give glory to
the Lord in verses 14-16 (compare Psalm 29, which takes the thunderstorm
as an occasion to give glory to the Lord).

Only two verses give a reason for the desolation of the earth. Verses 5-6
lay the blame on humanity. The offenses are stated in very general terms:
they have transgressed laws, broken an everlasting covenant (v. 5). The
covenant in question is not necessarily the one made with Moses at Sinai.
The phrase "everlasting covenant" (our text reads "ancient covenant") is used
in Gen 9:16 for the covenant with Noah, which was a covenant with all
peoples, not just Israel. The disruption of the earth, then, may be due to
a breach of natural law. The underlying idea is that the order of nature is
directly affected by human behavior. This idea was common in ancient Israel, especially in the temple cult. We can appreciate it anew in modern times
as we observe the effects of technological progress on the environment or
contemplate the threat to nature from the development of nuclear power.

Woe is me! The traitors betray:
with treachery have the traitors betrayed!
[17]Terror, pit, and trap
are upon you, inhabitant of the earth;
[18]He who flees at the sound of terror
will fall into the pit;
He who climbs out of the pit
will be caught in the trap.
For the windows on high will be opened
and the foundations of the earth will
shake.

[19]The earth will burst asunder,
the earth will be shaken apart,
the earth will be convulsed.
[20]The earth will reel like a drunkard,
and it will sway like a hut;
Its rebellion will weigh it down,
until it falls, never to rise again."
[21]On that day the LORD will punish
the host of the heavens in the
heavens,
and the kings of the earth on the
earth.

The desolation of the earth redounds to the glory of God, but it is nonetheless a hardship for humanity. Verses 16b-20 evoke the sense of terror for
humanity in the manifestation of God's majesty (compare Amos 5:19 on the
impossibility of escaping from God's judgment; also, more directly, Jer
48:43-44). Verses 18b-19 describe the destruction of the world. The "windows on high" will let in the floodwaters that have been restrained since creation (compare Jer 4:23-26, where the whole earth is returned to its primeval
state and creation is undone). Both in Isa 18-20 and in Jeremiah this total
destruction is still in the future. It should not be taken literally as a prediction of the end of the world but as a vivid metaphorical way of conveying
a sense of impending desolation.

24:21-23 The final judgment. The last oracle in chapter 24 picks up explicitly the motif of "the day of the Lord." The judgment described, however,
has no parallel in the Old Testament, for it includes the punishment of the
host of heaven—that is, the stars, which were regarded as angels (see Judg
5:20) or as pagan gods (Deut 4:19; Jer 8:2). The story of rebellious angels
who are then punished by God is told in detail in the apocalyptic book of
1 Enoch in the second century B.C.E. This passage in Isaiah raises the possibility that some mythological notions that first appear in post-biblical Jewish literature had in fact been current at a much earlier time.

The parallel punishment of the host of the heavens and the kings of the
earth suggests that the two are closely related. The kings of the earth have
their heavenly patrons (compare the notion of guardian angels), who are the
real source of their power. This idea was widespread in antiquity. We will
meet it again in Isa 36-37.

The culmination of the entire "day of the Lord" is that the Lord of hosts
will reign on Mount Zion. The basic concepts in these oracles are drawn from
Jerusalem cult traditions. The goal is the veneration of God on Mount Zion.
This goal is to be reached through widespread destruction that will bring
all peoples, including the Jews, to their knees. It is assumed, however, that

²²They will be gathered together
  like prisoners into a pit;
They will be shut up in a dungeon,
  and after many days they will be pun-
    ished.
²³Then the moon will blush
  and the sun grow pale,
For the LORD of hosts will reign
  on Mount Zion and in Jerusalem,
  glorious in the sight of his elders.

25 ¹O LORD, you are my God,
  I will extol you and praise your
    name;
For you have fulfilled your wonderful
    plans of old,
  faithful and true.
²For you have made the city a heap,
  the fortified city a ruin;
The castle of the insolent is a city no
    more,

nor ever to be rebuilt.
³Therefore a strong people will honor
    you,
  fierce nations will fear you.
⁴For you are a refuge to the poor,
  a refuge to the needy in distress;
Shelter from the rain,
  shade from the heat.
As with the cold rain,
⁵ as with the desert heat,
    even so you quell the uproar of the
      wanton.
⁶On this mountain the LORD of hosts
  will provide for all peoples
A feast of rich food and choice wines,
  juicy, rich food and pure, choice
    wines.
⁷On this mountain he will destroy
  the veil that veils all peoples,
The web that is woven over all nations;

life will go on on earth. God is to be glorified in Jerusalem, not in heaven. Christian readers may have difficulty with the prophet's insistence on the particular place, Mount Zion. They can at least appreciate some of the implications. The God of Mount Zion is the God of all the earth, and the frailty of humankind is the converse of the majesty of God.

25:1-5 A hymn of thanksgiving. This short hymn would appear to be written to celebrate the fall of a particular city (the most obvious candidate is Babylon). The lack of specificity, however, makes it possible to reapply it to any other city, or even to take it as a general affirmation of God's ability to upset the status quo (see the song of Hannah in 1 Sam 2).

25:6-8 The final banquet. The image of the great banquet is taken from ancient mythology and has a long history in the folklore of the world. The motif is developed in the "wedding feast of the lamb" in Rev 19 (see also the parable of the great supper in Matt 22:2-14; Luke 14:16-24). The banquet suggests a celebration after the victory is won. In this case the banquet is given "on this mountain," presumably Mount Zion. It is, however, a feast for all peoples, in accordance with the tradition that all the nations would flock to Zion. The feast is described with mouth-watering vividness. This is not the heaven of a disembodied soul but probably reflects the desire of impoverished people for a bountiful meal. The salvation desired goes beyond this, however. God will destroy death forever. In Canaanite mythology, Death (Mot) was the name of a god, the opponent of Baal, god of fertility. The prophet is probably alluding to that myth. The resurrection of those

8 he will destroy death forever.
The Lord GOD will wipe away
    the tears from all faces;
The reproach of his people he will re-
    move
    from the whole earth; for the LORD
    has spoken.
9   On that day it will be said:
"Behold our God, to whom we looked
    to save us!
This is the LORD for whom we looked;
let us rejoice and be glad that he has
    saved us!"
10For the hand of the LORD will rest on this
    mountain,
    but Moab will be trodden down
    as a straw is trodden down in the
    mire.
11He will stretch forth his hands in Moab
    as a swimmer extends his hands to
    swim;
He will bring low their pride
    as his hands sweep over them.
12The high-walled fortress he will raze,
    and strike it down level with the
    earth, with the very dust.

26 The Divine Vindicator. 1On that
day they will sing this song in the
land of Judah:

"A strong city have we;
    he sets up walls and ramparts to
    protect us.
2Open up the gates
    to let in a nation that is just,
    one that keeps faith.
3A nation of firm purpose you keep in
    peace;
    in peace, for its trust in you."
4Trust in the LORD forever!
    For the LORD is an eternal Rock.
5He humbles those in high places,
    and the lofty city he brings down;
He tumbles it to the ground,
    levels it with the dust.
6It is trampled underfoot by the needy,
    by the footsteps of the poor.
7The way of the just is smooth;
    the path of the just you make level.
8Yes, for your way and your judgments,
    O LORD,
    we look to you;
Your name and your title
    are the desire of our souls,
9My soul yearns for you in the night,
    yes, my spirit within me keeps vigil
    for you;
When your judgment dawns upon the
    earth,

who have already died is *not* implied here. Rather, the point is that God will ultimately remove every threat that hangs over humanity, including the ultimate one. God will also remove all sorrow and the humiliation of the Jewish people during the Exile. The prophet may have hoped for such salvation after the end of the Exile, but the destruction of death remains, inevitably, a distant horizon. Christianity transferred the land without tears to heaven; for Judaism it remains a utopian ideal for life on earth. (For the destruction of death, see Rev 20:14).

25:9-12 Oracle against Moab. The specific reference to Moab here is usually taken to indicate a date after the Exile when relations were bad between Judea and her neighbors. (The oracle in Isa 24:17-18 is cited as an oracle against Moab in Jer 48:43-44.) Moab was located east of the Dead Sea.

26:1-19 Song of trust. Isa 26 begins as a standard psalm of trust in God, affirming that God vindicates the life of the righteous poor. Verses 11-19 proceed to contrast the other lords who have ruled over Israel with the people of God. The other lords are dead; they cannot rise. The allusion here is

the world's inhabitants learn justice.
[10]The wicked man, spared, does not learn justice;
in an upright land he acts perversely,
and sees not the majesty of the LORD.
[11]O LORD, your hand is uplifted,
but they behold it not;
Let them be shamed when they see your zeal for your people:
let the fire prepared for your enemies consume them.
[12]O LORD, you mete out peace to us,
for it is you who have accomplished all we have done.
[13]O LORD, our God, other lords than you have ruled us;
it is from you only that we can call upon your name.
[14]Dead they are, they have no life,
shades that cannot rise;
For you have punished and destroyed them,
and wiped out all memory of them.
[15]You have increased the nation, O LORD,
increased the nation to your own glory,
and extended far all the borders of the land.
[16]O LORD, oppressed by your punishment,
we cried out in anguish under your chastising.
[17]As a woman about to give birth
writhes and cries out in her pains,
so were we in your presence, O LORD.
[18]We conceived and writhed in pain,
giving birth to wind;
Salvation we have not achieved for the earth,
the inhabitants of the world cannot bring it forth.
[19]But your dead shall live, their corpses shall rise;
awake and sing, you who lie in the dust.
For your dew is a dew of light,
and the land of shades gives birth.

Day of the Lord: Reward and Punishment

[20]Go, my people, enter your chambers,
and close your doors behind you;
Hide yourselves for a brief moment,

probably to Babylon, which was indeed dead as a world power. The Israelites had long labored in vain, failing to achieve salvation. But now, "your dead shall live, their corpses shall rise" (26:19). Some scholars take this verse as the earliest attestation of belief in resurrection in the Hebrew Bible. In view of the context, however, that is unlikely. The point is that Babylonian power is broken and will not be revived. Israelite power, which had been broken, will be revived. The resurrection involved is probably another formulation of the increase of the nation noted in verse 15 (compare Ezekiel's vision of the valley full of dry bones in Ezek 37, which is explicitly interpreted to refer to "the whole house of Israel"). It is the resurrection of a nation through a new generation, not the resuscitation of those who are already dead. Of course, the use of resurrection language to describe the restoration of the Jewish people helped to pave the way for the eventual emergence of a belief in the resurrection of the dead (which is first attested in Judaism in the second century B.C.E.).

26:20-21 Hiding from the wrath. This short oracle suggests that Israel (or perhaps the remnant) is exempt from the wrath of God. The idea that some people can hide from the wrath recalls the Exodus story in which the

until the wrath is past.
²¹See, the LORD goes forth from his place,
    to punish the wickedness of the
    earth's inhabitants;
The earth will reveal the blood upon
    her,
    and no longer conceal her slain.

27 ¹ On that day,
The LORD will punish with his
    sword
that is cruel, great, and strong,
Leviathan the fleeing serpent,
    Leviathan the coiled serpent;
    and he will slay the dragon that is in
    the sea.

Lord passes over those houses that have been properly marked (Exod 12). For God going forth to judge the world, the reader should compare the theophanies in Judg 5; Deut 33; Hab 3; also Psalm 98. The prophet also assures the people that the time of God's wrath is a brief moment. If they can wait out the bad time, they will yet be glorified. This idea also plays an important role in Second Isaiah's explanation of the Exile.

27:1 Leviathan. A number of passages in the Bible allude to a battle between God and a monster (variously called a dragon or Rahab; see Isa 51:9; Job 26:12). Usually this battle is in the past. The story of this battle is not told in Genesis or Exodus, and we have only recently come to understand the allusion. The Canaanite myths (which were discovered at Ugarit in northern Syria in 1929) include the story of a battle between the god Baal and the Sea. Associated with the Sea are monsters called Lotan, the dragon, and the crooked serpent. All these are probably the same figure, called by different names. The dragon is a symbol of chaos—all the forces opposed to peace and order. The battle between a god and a dragon was a Canaanite story and symbolized the victory of life and order over chaos. For the Canaanites, Baal was the god who slew the monster and made civilized life possible. When the biblical authors referred to this story, they substituted Yahweh for Baal. For them, it was their God who slew the dragon when the world was created or Israel was led out of Egypt.

Leviathan in Isa 27:1 is the Lotan of Canaanite myth and another name for the sea dragon. This passage, however, suggests that he has not yet been slain. The decisive battle for the welfare and salvation of the world has not yet been won. It remains in the future, to be fought on the "day of the Lord." This expectation of a decisive action by God in the future becomes increasingly prominent in later biblical writings and in the apocalyptic literature. The symbolism of the sea monsters plays a prominent part in Dan 7 and in the Book of Revelation, especially chapters 12 and 13.

The symbol of the monster, Leviathan, is exceptionally powerful. Traditional Christianity would relate this figure to Satan, but the original symbol could be used for any threat to human welfare. "Doing battle with the monster" remains a useful metaphor for our various struggles in life.

2   On that day—
The pleasant vineyard, sing about it!
3   I, the LORD, am its keeper,
    I water it every moment;
Lest anyone harm it,
    night and day I guard it.
4I am not angry,
    but if I were to find briers and thorns,
In battle I should march against them;
    I should burn them all.
8Expunging and expelling, I should
    strive against them,
    carrying them off with my cruel wind
    in time of storm.

6In days to come Jacob shall take root,
    Israel shall sprout and blossom,
    covering all the world with fruit.
7Is he to be smitten as his smiter was
    smitten?
    or slain as his slayer was slain?

5Or shall he cling to me for refuge?
He must make peace with me;
    peace shall he make with me!

9This, then, shall be the expiation of
    Jacob's guilt,
this the whole fruit of the removal of
    his sin:
He shall pulverize all the stones of the
    altars
    like pieces of chalk;
    no sacred poles or incense altars
    shall stand.
10For the fortified city shall be desolate,
    an abandoned pasture, a forsaken
    wilderness,
    where calves shall browse and lie.
Its boughs shall be destroyed,
11   its branches shall wither and be
    broken off,
    and women shall come to build a fire
    with them.
This is not an understanding people;
    therefore their maker shall not spare
    them,
    nor shall he who formed them have
    mercy on them.
12   On that day,
The LORD shall beat out the grain
    between the Euphrates and the Wadi
    of Egypt,
    and you shall be gleaned one by one,

27:2-13 The restoration of Israel. This section of Isaiah concludes with
a series of oracles introduced by the phrase "On that day." The first picks
up the motif of the vineyard from Isa 5. Now Yahweh is no longer angry.
Briers and thorns are no longer means of punishment; rather, God will burn
them.

The restoration of Israel is conditional, however, on cultic purity—
essentially observance of the reform carried out by King Josiah in 621 B.C.E.
(see 2 Kgs 22–23), which involved the destruction of altars and places of worship outside of Jerusalem, in accordance with the law of Deut 12.

The "fortified city" (v. 10) and "not an understanding people" (v. 11)
would seem to refer to a specific city and people. Many scholars identify
the city in this case as Samaria. The allusions to Jacob and Israel, then, should
be read as "the northern kingdom," and the implication would be that Israel
should find its center in Jerusalem and not in Samaria. The passage is obscure, however. Both its origin and its reference are uncertain.

The last two oracles refer to the gathering in of Jews from the Diaspora.
As we have come to expect in the Book of Isaiah, they are to worship on
the holy mountain in Jerusalem. Part of the editor's program was apparently

O sons of Israel.
¹³ On that day,
A great trumpet shall blow,
 and the lost in the land of Assyria
 and the outcasts in the land of Egypt
Shall come and worship the LORD
 on the holy mountain, in Jerusalem.

V: THE LORD ALONE,
ISRAEL'S AND JUDAH'S SALVATION

The Fate of Samaria

28 ¹Woe to the majestic garland
 of the drunkard Ephraim,
To the fading blooms of his glorious
 beauty,
 on the head of him who is stupefied
with wine.
²Behold, the LORD has a strong one and a
 mighty,
 who, like a downpour of hail, a destructive storm,
Like a flood of water, great and over-
 flowing,
 levels to the ground with violence;
³With feet that will trample
 the majestic garland of the drunkard
 Ephraim.
⁴The fading blooms of his glorious
 beauty
 on the head of the fertile valley
Will be like an early fig before summer:
 when a man sees it,

to reunite the whole people with Mount Zion as the place of worship for all. In this respect he was probably in continuity with Isaiah of Jerusalem.

POLITICS AND SALVATION

Isa 28:1–33:24

With chapter 28 we return to a cluster of oracles from Isaiah himself. The core of this cluster comes from the time of Hezekiah's decision to revolt against Assyria in 701 B.C.E. A major factor in Hezekiah's decision to revolt was the hope that Egypt would support the various rebel states. Many of Isaiah's prophecies are concerned with the folly of that hope.

These chapters have come to us through the hands of an editor. The oracles are arranged so that judgment and salvation alternate. Many of the oracles of salvation may come from a later time. Nearly all of chapters 32–33 consist of later material. The final editing of this material probably took place after the Babylonian Exile.

28:1-4 The fall of Samaria. The first oracle of this section comes from an earlier period of Isaiah's career, before the fall of Samaria in 722 B.C.E. It is included here partly to ensure that the prophet's word will be seen to address all of Israel and partly because drunkenness is also a theme of the following oracle in verses 7-22. The oracle in verses 1-4 recalls Isaiah's preaching in Isa 5 and that of the prophet Amos. The downfall of Samaria comes from the lifestyle of the upper classes, symbolized by their drunkenness. The "garland" in verse 1 refers to the city of Samaria, perched like a crown on a hill.

he picks and swallows it at once.
⁵On that day the LORD of hosts
  will be a glorious crown
And a brilliant diadem
  to the remnant of his people,
⁶A spirit of justice
  to him who sits in judgment,
And strength to those
  who turn back the battle at the gate.

Against Judah

⁷But these also stagger from wine
  and stumble from strong drink:
Priest and prophet stagger from strong
    drink,
  overpowered by wine;
Led astray by strong drink
  staggering in their visions,
  tottering when giving judgment.
⁸Yes, all the tables
  are covered with filthy vomit,
  with no place left clean.
⁹"To whom would he impart knowledge?
To whom would he convey the
    message?
To those just weaned from milk,
  those taken from the breast? ¹⁰For he
  says,

'Command on command, command on
    command,
  rule on rule, rule on rule,
  here a little, there a little!' "
¹¹Yes, with stammering lips and in a
    strange language
  he will speak to this people
¹² to whom he said:
This is the resting place,
  give rest to the weary;
Here is repose—
  but they would not listen.
¹³So for them the word of the LORD shall
    be:
  "Command on command, command
    on command,
Rule on rule, rule on rule,
  here a little, there a little!"
So that when they walk, they stumble
    backward,
  broken, ensnared, and captured.
¹⁴Therefore, hear the word of the LORD,
    you arrogant,
  who rule this people in Jerusalem:
¹⁵Because you say, "We have made a
    covenant with death,
  and with the nether world we have
    made a pact;

28:5-6 The remnant. These verses are the work of an editor who wants to give a positive connotation to the image of a crown. The remnant here has a purely positive meaning. For the prophet Isaiah it was always ambiguous.

28:7-22 Judah's covenant with death. Verses 7-13 refer to Isaiah's dispute with the priests and the other prophets. The heavy drinking may have been in the context of a cultic celebration of Canaanite origin. People drank themselves into a stupor in a celebration of fellowship with the dead. It was an expensive practice that only the rich could afford. Whether Isaiah is referring to this ritual or not, the drunkenness of the priests implies social irresponsibility.

Verse 9 is presumably a quotation of Isaiah's opponents. In verse 10 they mock his preaching as if it were the stammering of a child. (The Hebrew makes no real sense.) Isaiah retorts that his speech sounds strange because they do not listen (see Isa 6:9 and, more directly, Ezek 3:5-9). The word of the Lord becomes nonsense to them, so that they stumble without guidance.

When the overwhelming scourge
 passes,
 it will not reach us;
For we have made lies our refuge,
 and in falsehood we have found a hiding place,"—
16   Therefore, thus says the Lord GOD:
See, I am laying a stone in Zion,
 a stone that has been tested,
A precious cornerstone as a sure foundation;
 he who puts his faith in it shall not be shaken.
17I will make of right a measuring line,
 of justice a level.—
Hail shall sweep away the refuge of lies,
 and waters shall flood the hiding place.

18Your covenant with death shall be canceled
 and your pact with the nether world shall not stand.
When the overwhelming scourge passes,
 you shall be trampled down by it.
19Whenever it passes, it shall take you;
 morning after morning it shall pass,
By day and by night;
 terror alone shall convey the message.
20For the bed shall be too short to stretch out in,
 and the cover too narrow to wrap in.
21For the LORD shall rise up as on Mount Perazim,
 bestir himself as in the Valley of Gibeon,
To carry out his work, his singular work,

Verses 14-15 are addressed to the rulers of Jerusalem, probably including the religious leaders. They are arrogant because they think they are secure. The "covenant with death" probably refers to an alliance with Egypt. The rulers think that the scourge of Assyria will not touch them because of this alliance. Isaiah, however, sees it as a covenant with death. Death (Mot) was the name of the Canaanite god, enemy of Baal, the god of fertility. Egypt, the traditional enemy of Israel, is called "Death" here, as it is given the name of another Canaanite deity, Rahab, in Isa 30:7. The point is that the attempt to secure life ends in death (see the story of Adam and Eve, and also Hos 13:1, where the Israelites who worship Baal find Mot [Death] instead). Isaiah says that the rulers have made lies their refuge. The lies are the double-talk inherent in diplomacy, but also the hope for Egyptian protection, which was only an illusion.

The cornerstone that God lays in Zion (v. 16) is either God or righteousness and justice. It implies a reference to the Davidic covenant, but the security of Zion depends on its adherence to justice (compare the oracle to Ahaz in Isa 7:9: "Unless your faith is firm you shall not be firm"). Those who trust in anything other than God will be swept away by the flood of Assyria (see Isa 8:8). The saying about the short bed in verse 20 means that there will be no place to rest or hide. The Assyrian invasion is the "strange deed" of God, just as surely as David's victory over the Philistines at Mount Perazim (2 Sam 5:17-25) or Joshua's victory over Gibeon when the sun stood still (Josh 10:1-15). The oracle ends with a definitive assurance that Isaiah has heard of the coming destruction directly from God.

to perform his deed, his strange deed.
²²Now, be arrogant no more
  lest your bonds be tightened,
For I have heard from the Lord, the God
  of hosts,
  the destruction decreed for the whole
  earth.
²³Give ear and hear my voice,
  pay attention and listen to what I say:
²⁴Is the plowman forever plowing,
  always loosening and harrowing his
  land for planting?
²⁵When he has leveled the surface,
  does he not scatter gith and sow
  cumin,
Put in wheat and barley,
  with spelt as its border?
²⁶He has learned this rule,
  instructed by his God.
²⁷Gith is not threshed with a sledge,
  nor does a cartwheel roll over cumin.
But gith is beaten out with a staff,
  and cumin crushed for food with a
  rod.
²⁸No, he does not thresh it unendingly,
  nor does he crush it
  with his noisy cartwheels and horses.

²⁹This too comes from the Lord of hosts;
  wonderful is his counsel and great his
  wisdom.

The Fall of Jerusalem

29 ¹Woe to Ariel, Ariel,
  the city where David encamped!
Add year to year,
  let the feasts come round.
²But I will bring distress upon Ariel,
  with mourning and grief.
You shall be to me like Ariel,
³ I will encamp like David against
  you;
I will encircle you with outposts
  and set up siege works against you.
⁴Prostrate you shall speak from the
  earth,
  and from the base dust your words
  shall come.
Your voice shall be like a ghost's from
  the earth,
  and your words like chirping from the
  dust.
⁵The horde of your arrogant shall be like
  fine dust,

28:23-29 A parable of salvation. The severe proclamation of judgment is followed by a promise of relief. The argument is based on analogy from nature: there is a season for everything, destruction cannot go on forever. Whether Isaiah spoke this oracle is disputed. It accords well with his overall message. He never predicted that Judah would be left without any remnant. It is unlikely that he delivered this oracle together with the preceding one, since it would have undermined the threat, but he may well have spoken it later, when the Assyrian invasion was underway or already past. An editor placed it here to show that the threat of destruction was ultimately modified and should not be taken as final.

29:1-8 Ariel, Ariel. Ariel is evidently a name for Jerusalem. Its meaning and origin are obscure. It may be derived from a word meaning "altar."

Verses 1-5a represent God as attacking Jerusalem (presumably through the Assyrians) just as David did long ago. Verse 1 gives the impression that the festivals are observed in a mindless manner and to no avail. Verse 4 vividly describes how Jerusalem will be brought low, but it stops short of saying that the city will be captured.

the horde of the tyrants like flying
chaff.
Then suddenly, in an instant,
6   you shall be visited by the Lord of
hosts,
With thunder, earthquake, and great
noise,
whirlwind, storm, and the flame of
consuming fire.
7Then like a dream,
a vision in the night,
Shall be the horde of all the nations
who war against Ariel
with all the earthworks of her be-
siegers.
8As when a hungry man dreams he is eating
and awakens with an empty stomach,
Or when a thirsty man dreams he is
drinking
and awakens faint and dry,
So shall the horde of all the nations be,
who make war against Zion.

Blindness and Perversity

9Be irresolute, stupefied;
blind yourselves and stay blind!
Be drunk, but not from wine,
stagger, but not from strong drink!
10For the Lord has poured out on you a
spirit of deep sleep.
He has shut your eyes [the prophets]
and covered your heads [the seers].

11For you the revelation of all this has
become like the words of a sealed scroll.
When it is handed to one who can read,
with the request, "Read this," he replies,
"I cannot; it is sealed." 12When it is
handed to one who cannot read, with the
request, "Read this," he replies, "I cannot read."

13   The Lord said:
Since this people draws near with words
only
and honors me with their lips alone,
though their hearts are far from me,

The sudden visitation by God in verse 6 is ambiguous here. On the one
hand, it completes the humiliation of Jerusalem; on the other hand, it is also
a saving act. The enemy will be frustrated at the last moment and will van-
ish like a dream of the night. This passage strongly resembles the Zion ideology presented in the psalms. According to Ps 48:5-6,

> . . . the kings assemble,
>   they come on together;
> They also see, and at once are stunned,
>   terrified, routed.

The psalm attests the belief in the inviolability of Zion, a popular belief in
Jerusalem that was later sharply criticized by Jeremiah (Jer 7:4). Many scholars question whether Isaiah would have endorsed such a belief. Yet, we have
found throughout that Isaiah's message was double-edged. First, Judah would
be brought to its knees, but it would not be utterly destroyed. Isaiah modi-
fies the Zion theology by insisting that Jerusalem is not protected from humiliation. The "strange deed" (28:21) of the Lord, then, includes both
extensive destruction and ultimate deliverance, and is presumably meant to
teach Judah a severe lesson.

29:9-16 Criticism of the "wise." These verses continue the critique of
28:7-22. The blindness of the leaders recalls the prophecy of Isa 6:9-10. The

And their reverence for me has become routine observance of the precepts of men,

[14]Therefore I will again deal with this people

in surprising and wondrous fashion:

The wisdom of its wise men shall perish and the understanding of its prudent men be hid.

[15]Woe to those who would hide their plans

too deep for the LORD!

Who work in the dark, saying,

"Who sees us, or who knows us?"

[16]Your perversity is as though the potter were taken to be the clay:

As though what is made should say of its maker,

"He made me not!"

Or the vessel should say of the potter,

"He does not understand."

Redemption

[17]But a very little while,

and Lebanon shall be changed into an orchard,

and the orchard be regarded as a forest!

[18]On that day the deaf shall hear

the words of a book;

And out of gloom and darkness,

the eyes of the blind shall see.

[19]The lowly will ever find joy in the LORD,

and the poor rejoice in the Holy One of Israel.

[20]For the tyrant will be no more

and the arrogant will have gone;

All who are alert to do evil will be cut off,

[21] those whose mere word condemns a man,

Who ensnare his defender at the gate,

and leave the just man with an empty claim.

[22]Therefore thus says the LORD,

the God of the house of Jacob,

who redeemed Abraham:

Now Jacob shall have nothing to be ashamed of,

nor shall his face grow pale.

[23]When his children see

the work of my hands in his midst,

They shall keep my name holy;

they shall reverence the Holy One of Jacob,

and be in awe of the God of Israel.

[24]Those who err in spirit shall acquire understanding,

and those who find fault shall receive instruction.

Futile Alliance with Egypt

30 [1]Woe to the rebellious children, says the LORD,

reasons for the criticism are twofold: superficial worship (v. 13; compare Matt 15:8; Mark 7:6) and the attempt of the king's advisers to control their destiny by devious diplomacy. Isaiah's ideal of simple submission to the plan of God would, of course, eliminate Judah's ambitions as a state.

29:17-24 Prophecy of salvation. In some respects, the predominant optimism of this prophecy is closer in spirit to Second Isaiah than to Isaiah of Jerusalem (compare 29:18 with 42:7). Yet, much of what it anticipates concerns the internal reform of Judah, especially the removal of the arrogant rulers. This theme follows well enough on verses 9-16. It may be that an original oracle of Isaiah was recast by the editor to provide a counterpart to the negative oracles of verses 9-16.

30:1-18 Alliance with Egypt. Isaiah again castigates the Judeans for relying on international intrigue and especially on the promise of Egyptian help. The

Who carry out plans that are not mine,
who weave webs that are not inspired
by me,
adding sin upon sin.
²They go down to Egypt,
but my counsel they do not seek.
They find their strength in Pharaoh's
protection
and take refuge in Egypt's shadow;
³Pharaoh's protection shall be your
shame,
and refuge in Egypt's shadow your
disgrace.
⁴When their princes are at Zoan
and their messengers reach Hanes,
⁵All shall be ashamed
of a people that gain them nothing,
Neither help nor benefit,
but only shame and reproach.
⁶   [Oracle on the Beasts of the Negeb]
Through the distressed and troubled
land
of the lioness and roaring lion,
of the viper and flying saraph,
They carry their riches on the backs of
asses
and their treasures on the humps of
camels

To a people good for nothing,
⁷ to Egypt whose help is futile and
vain.
Therefore I call her
"Rahab quelled."
⁸Now come, write it on a tablet they can
keep,
inscribe it in a record;
That it may be in future days
an eternal witness:
⁹This is a rebellious people,
deceitful children,
Children who refuse
to obey the law of the LORD.
¹⁰They say to the seers, "Have no visions";
to the prophets, "Do not descry for
us what is right;
speak flatteries to us, conjure up illusions.
¹¹Out of the way! Out of our path!
Let us hear no more
of the Holy One of Israel."
¹²Therefore, thus says the Holy One of
Israel:
Because you reject this word,
And put your trust in what is crooked
and devious,

gifts given to Egypt are wasted. Egypt is called "Rahab," a name for the chaos monster (see Job 26:12), but it is a subdued Rahab, not only evil but useless. The prophet is irate at the unwillingness of the people to listen to his own message or to consider the Holy One as a factor in their plans. The king's counselors found prophets useful enough when they spoke flattery and were willing to spread propaganda; the prophet who had an independent point of view was merely a nuisance.

Isaiah's message to Hezekiah was essentially the same as his advice to Ahaz: "By waiting and by calm you shall be saved." First, they should not provoke the Assyrians by revolting. Second, they should not compound the problem by alliances and attempts at resistance. Isaiah makes no allowance for national pride, nor even for the natural instinct to provide for one's own protection. The *trust* is that God will protect them, not indeed from all harm, but from being wiped out. This passive approach might mean accepting much suffering, but Isaiah could validly argue that the alternatives were worse. They could not hope to flee from the Assyrians. Patient trust here becomes

and depend on it,
¹³This guilt of yours shall be
  like a descending rift
Bulging out in a high wall
  whose crash comes suddenly, in an
    instant.
¹⁴It crashes like a potter's jar
  smashed beyond rescue,
And among its fragments cannot be
  found
  a sherd to scoop fire from the hearth
  or dip water from the cistern.
¹⁵For thus said the Lord GOD,
  the Holy One of Israel:
By waiting and by calm you shall be
  saved,
  in quiet and in trust your strength lies.
  But this you did not wish.
¹⁶"No," you said,
  "Upon horses we will flee."
  —Very well, flee!
  "Upon swift steeds we will ride."
  —Not so swift as your pursuers.
¹⁷A thousand shall tremble at the threat
  of one;
  if five threaten you, you shall flee,
Until you are left like a flagstaff on the
  mountaintop,
  like a flag on the hill.
¹⁸Yet the LORD is waiting to show you
  favor,
  and he rises to pity you;
For the LORD is a God of justice:
  blessed are all who wait for him!
¹⁹O people of Zion, who dwell in Jerusalem,

no more will you weep;
He will be gracious to you when you cry
  out,
  as soon as he hears he will answer
    you.
²⁰The Lord will give you the bread you
  need
  and the water for which you thirst.
No longer will your Teacher hide himself,
  but with your own eyes you shall see
    your Teacher,
²¹While from behind, a voice shall sound
  in your ears:
  "This is the way; walk in it,"
  when you would turn to the right or
    to the left.
²²And you shall consider unclean your
  silver-plated idols
  and your gold-covered images;
You shall throw them away like filthy
  rags
  to which you say, "Begone!"

Zion's Future Prosperity

²³He will give rain for the seed
  that you sow in the ground,
And the wheat that the soil produces
  will be rich and abundant.
On that day your cattle will graze
  in spacious meadows;
²⁴The oxen and the asses that till the
  ground
  will eat silage tossed to them
  with shovel and pitchfork.
²⁵Upon every high mountain and lofty hill

the cornerstone (Isa 28:16) of the hope for salvation in Zion. We may compare Isaiah's stance with the ethic of nonresistance attributed to Jesus in the
Sermon on the Mount (Matt 5:38-42). We should emphasize, however, that
for Isaiah nonresistance was a political tactic that might lessen the danger
of outright destruction.

30:19-26 Salvation for Zion. Verses 19-26, probably the work of an editor, expand on the idea that God is willing to show favor. The concern for
the destruction of idols (v. 22) and the transformation of the high places (v.
23) point to the time of King Josiah's reform, when the cultic sites outside
Jerusalem were destroyed (2 Kgs 23). Verse 21, "This is the way . . . ," is

there will be streams of running
   water.
On the day of the great slaughter,
   when the towers fall,
²⁶The light of the moon will be like that
   of the sun
   and the light of the sun will be seven
      times greater
   [like the light of seven days].
On the day the LORD binds up the
   wounds of his people,
   he will heal the bruises left by his
      blows.

Divine Judgment on Assyria

²⁷See the name of the LORD coming from
   afar
   in burning wrath, with lowering
      clouds!
His lips are filled with fury,
   his tongue is like a consuming fire;
²⁸His breath, like a flood in a ravine
   that reaches suddenly to the neck,
Will winnow the nations with a destructive winnowing,
   and with repeated winnowings will he
      battle against them
   [and a bridle on the jaws of the
      peoples to send them astray].
³⁰The LORD will make his glorious voice
   heard,

and let it be seen how his arm
   descends
In raging fury and flame of consuming
   fire,
   in driving storm and hail.
³¹When the LORD speaks, Assyria will be
   shattered,
   as he strikes with the rod;
³²While at every sweep of the rod
   which the LORD will bring down on
      him in punishment,
²⁹You will sing
   as on a night when a feast is observed,
And be merry of heart,
   as one marching along with a flute
Toward the mountain of the LORD,
   toward the rock of Israel,
   accompanied by the timbrels and
      lyres.
³³For the pyre has long been ready,
   prepared for the king;
Broad and deep it is piled
   with dry grass and wood in abun-
      dance,
And the breath of the LORD, like a
   stream of sulphur,
   will set it afire.

Against the Egyptian Alliance

31 ¹Woe to those who go down to
   Egypt for help,

the fulfillment of the promise of Isa 2:3 that God would "instruct us in his
ways."

30:27-33 Judgment on Assyria. This oracle, too, may be a later addi-
tion, from the time when Assyria fell to the Babylonians in 612 B.C.E. The idea
that Assyria would eventually be destroyed had its precedent in Isa 10. The
manifestation of God in the thunderstorm is the image used throughout Isaiah
for destruction, whether of Israel or of Assyria. The prophet points out that
the oppressors of history eventually fall. Even though the prophets use historical crises as occasions to press for the reform of their own people, it is important that they do not thereby endorse the actions of the superpowers.

31:1-3 Flesh and spirit. Yet another indictment of the alliance with Egypt
puts the matter in a new way: the Egyptians are human and not divine, their
horses are flesh and not spirit. The contrast here is not between body and
soul but between human power and divine power. The Egyptians have only

who depend upon horses;
Who put their trust in chariots because
of their number,
and in horsemen because of their
combined power,
But look not to the Holy One of Israel
nor seek the LORD!
²Yet he too is wise and will bring disaster;
he will not turn from what he has
threatened to do.
He will rise up against the house of the
wicked
and against those who help evildoers.
³The Egyptians are men, not God,
their horses are flesh, not spirit;
When the LORD stretches forth his hand,
the helper shall stumble, the one
helped shall fall,
and both of them shall perish together.
⁴   Thus says the LORD to me:
As a lion or a lion cub
growling over its prey,
With a band of shepherds
assembled against it,
Is neither frightened by their shouts
nor disturbed by their noise,

So shall the LORD of hosts come down
to wage war upon the mountain and
hill of Zion.
⁵Like hovering birds, so the LORD of hosts
shall shield Jerusalem,
To protect and deliver,
to spare and rescue it.
⁶Return, O children of Israel, to him
whom you have utterly deserted. ⁷On
that day each one of you shall spurn his
sinful idols of silver and gold, which he
made with his hands.

Downfall of Assyria

⁸Assyria shall fall by a sword not wielded
by man,
no mortal sword shall devour him;
He shall flee before the sword,
and his young men shall be impressed
as laborers.
⁹He shall rush past his crag in panic,
and his princes shall flee in terror
from his standard.
Says the LORD who has a fire in Zion
and a furnace in Jerusalem.

The Kingdom of Justice

32 ¹See, a king will reign justly
and princes will rule rightly.

fallible human power; they are not supernatural and can work no miracles
to save Judah from Assyria. The point is that Judah overrates Egypt. Similarly the horses, a crucial element in the armaments for the day, are only
flesh; they cannot withstand what Isaiah sees as the plan of God. This contrast of flesh, as mere humanity, to the spirit or power of God will play an
important role in the theology of St. Paul in the New Testament.

31:4-6 Deliverance of Zion. As in the preceding chapters, an editor has
balanced the prophet's indictment with an oracle of salvation. The image
of God sheltering Jerusalem like a flock of birds fits well with the popular
Zion theology but is far too simple for Isaiah, who preached consistently
that only a remnant would survive. The reference to idols in verse 7 again
shows the concerns of King Josiah's reform.

31:8 Fall of Assyria. Like the preceding chapter, chapter 31 ends with
a prediction of the fall of Assyria, to set the record straight. When Assyria
did fall, the sword was wielded by the Babylonians, but a Jewish prophet
would still see that event as the work of the Lord.

²Each of them will be a shelter from the
wind,
a retreat from the rain.
They will be like streams of water in a
dry country,
like the shade of a great rock in a
parched land.
³The eyes of those who see will not be
closed;
the ears of those who hear will be
attentive.
⁴The flighty will become wise and
capable,
and the stutterers will speak fluently
and clearly.
⁵No more will the fool be called noble,
nor the trickster be considered honorable.
⁶For the fool speaks foolishly,
planning evil in his heart:
How to do wickedness,
to speak perversely against the LORD,
To let the hungry go empty
and the thirsty be without drink.
⁷And the trickster uses wicked trickery,
planning crimes:
How to ruin the poor with lies,

and the needy when they plead their
case.
⁸But the noble man plans noble things,
and by noble things he stands.

The Women of Jerusalem

⁹O complacent ladies, rise up and hear
my voice,
overconfident women, give heed to
my words.
¹⁰In a little more than a year
you overconfident ones will be
shaken;
The vintage will fail,
there will be no harvest.
¹¹Tremble, you who are complacent!
Shudder, you who are overconfident!
Strip yourselves bare,
with only a loincloth to cover you.
¹²Beat your breasts
for the pleasant fields, the fruitful
vine,
¹³And the soil of my people,
overgrown with thorns and briers;
For all the joyful houses,
the wanton city.
¹⁴Yes, the castle will be forsaken,

32:1-8 A just king. Unlike the messianic prophecies in Isa 9 and 11, this
passage does not refer explicitly to the Davidic line or the royal ideology;
therefore it has been thought to come from a later hand. It does presuppose
the existence of the monarchy, however, and so must be preexilic. The contrast of the fool and the noble is typical of the wisdom literature. Verse 3
would seem to deliberately revoke Isa 6:10. The concern of the passage is
with justice in the land, with feeding the hungry and giving drink to the
thirsty. It implies a criticism of the rulers of the day, who are branded as
fools for their neglect of the Lord and for social injustice. The oracle is in
continuity with the preaching of Isaiah, but the generalized references to the
fool and the trickster lack the specificity of a passage like Isa 5.

32:9-13 Prophecy of impending destruction. This passage picks up motifs from earlier prophecies of Isaiah (see the oracle against the women of
Jerusalem in 3:16-26 and the briers and thorns in 5:6; 7:23-24). Here, however, the address is to women of the countryside, in view of the references
to fields and harvest. It does not indict them for luxury but wants to alert
them to imminent danger. The occasion of this oracle is unknown.

the noisy city deserted;
¹⁹Down it comes, as trees come down in
the forest!
The city will be utterly laid low.
Hill and tower will become wasteland
forever
for wild asses to frolic in, and flocks
to pasture,
¹⁵Until the spirit from on high
is poured out on us.
Then will the desert become an orchard
and the orchard be regarded as a
forest.
¹⁶Right will dwell in the desert
and justice abide in the orchard.
¹⁷Justice will bring about peace;
right will produce calm and security.
¹⁸My people will live in peaceful country,
in secure dwellings and quiet resting
places.
²⁰Happy are you who sow beside every
stream,
and let the ox and the ass go freely!

Overthrow of Assyria

33 ¹Woe, O destroyer never destroyed,
O traitor never betrayed!
When you finish destroying, you will be
destroyed;
when wearied with betraying, you
will be betrayed.
²O LORD, have pity on us, for you we
wait.
Be our strength every morning,
our salvation in time of trouble!
³At the roaring sound, peoples flee;
when you rise in your majesty, nations are scattered.
⁴Men gather spoil as caterpillars are
gathered up;
they rush upon it like the onrush of
locusts.
⁵The LORD is exalted, enthroned on high;
he fills Zion with right and justice.
⁶That which makes her seasons lasting,
the riches that save her, are wisdom

32:14-20 A rustic utopia. The New American Bible has transposed verse 19 and placed it before verse 15, thereby altering the sense of the passage. In the Hebrew the transformation of the desert goes hand in hand with the destruction of the city. When the city is destroyed, the people will live in the quiet countryside, imbued with the spirit of the Lord. This passage does not accord well with either the message of Isaiah or with most of the tradition in this book, all of which had an important place for a purified Jerusalem in any final utopia (see especially 2:1-5, but also 33:17-24). The New American Bible solves the difficulty by moving the last verse and so allowing that the city may share in the restoration. Others suggest a different translation (for example, the "cities shall lie peaceful in the plain"—New English Bible), but even this contrasts with the exaltation of Zion in Isa 2. We may at least see some continuity between Isaiah's disdain for the luxury of the upper classes and the negative attitude toward the city here. The blooming of the desert appears again in 35:1 and 43:19-20.

33:1 Oracle against an enemy. This very brief oracle is addressed to Assyria or Babylon or some other enemy. The logic is the same as in Isa 10 or 30:27-33: the day of the oppressor will come.

33:2-16 Prayer for God's manifestation. This section is made up of smaller units that alternate between distress and hope for the manifestation

and knowledge;
the fear of the LORD is her treasure.
⁷See, the men of Ariel cry out in the streets,
the messengers of Shalem weep bitterly.
⁸The highways are desolate,
travelers have quit the paths,
Covenants are broken, their terms are spurned;
yet no man gives it a thought.
⁹The country languishes in mourning,
Lebanon withers with shame;
Sharon is like the steppe,
Bashan and Carmel are stripped bare.

¹⁰Now will I rise up, says the LORD,
now will I be exalted, now be lifted up.
¹¹You conceive dry grass, bring forth stubble;
my spirit shall consume you like fire.
¹²The peoples shall be as in a limekiln,
like brushwood cut down for burning in the fire.

¹³Hear, you who are far off, what I have done;
you who are near, acknowledge my might.
¹⁴On Zion sinners are in dread,
trembling grips the impious:
"Who of us can live with the consuming fire?
who of us can live with the everlasting flames?"
¹⁵He who practices virtue and speaks honestly,

who spurns what is gained by oppression,
Brushing his hands free of contact with a bribe,
stopping his ears lest he hear of bloodshed,
closing his eyes lest he look on evil—
¹⁶He shall dwell on the heights,
his stronghold shall be the rocky fastness,
his food and drink in steady supply.

Restoration of Zion

¹⁷Your eyes will see a king in his splendor,
they will look upon a vast land.
¹⁸Your mind will dwell on the terror:
"Where is he who counted, where is he who weighed?
Where is he who counted the towers?"
¹⁹To the people of alien tongue you will look no more,
the people of obscure speech,
stammering in a language not understood.
²⁰Look to Zion, the city of our festivals;
let your eyes see Jerusalem
as a quiet abode, a tent not to be struck,
Whose pegs will never be pulled up,
nor any of its ropes severed.
²²Indeed the LORD will be there with us, majestic;
yes, the LORD our judge, the LORD our lawgiver,
the LORD our king, he it is who will save us.

of God. Verses 2-4 pray for God to be revealed on Zion and terrify all enemies. Verses 7-9 describe the breakdown of the country. Verses 10-13 are an oracle proclaiming the theophany. Verse 14 states the initial human response: who of us can live with the consuming fire? The manifestation of God is terrifying even for God's own people. Verses 15-16 give the answer: the virtuous can stand in the presence of God. This whole passage would seem to be derived from a liturgy in the Jerusalem temple (see Psalm 24).

33:17-24 The restoration of Zion. This passage may well have concluded one edition of the prophecies of Isaiah. The editor promises a full restora-

²¹In a place of rivers and wide streams
  on which no boat is rowed,
  where no majestic ship passes,
²³The rigging hangs slack;
  it cannot hold the mast in place,
  nor keep the sail spread out.
Then the blind will divide great spoils
  and the lame will carry off the loot.
²⁴No one who dwells there will say, "I am
  sick";
  the people who live there will be for-
  given their guilt.

VI: THE LORD, ZION'S AVENGER

Judgment upon Edom

34 ¹Come near, O nations, and
  hear;
  be attentive, O peoples!
Let the earth and what fills it listen,
  the world and all it produces.
²The LORD is angry with all the nations
  and is wrathful against all their hosts;
  he has doomed them and given them
  over to slaughter.
³Their slain shall be cast out,
  their corpses shall send up a stench;
The mountains shall run with their
  blood,

⁴ and all the hills shall rot;
The heavens shall be rolled up like a
  scroll,
  and all their host shall wither away,
As the leaf wilts on the vine,
  or as the fig withers on the tree.
⁵When my sword has drunk its fill in the
  heavens,
  lo, it shall come down in judgment
  upon Edom, a people I have doomed.
⁶The LORD has a sword filled with blood,
  greasy with fat,
With the blood of lambs and goats,
  with the fat of rams' kidneys;
For the LORD has a sacrifice in Bozrah,
  a great slaughter in the land of Edom.
⁷Wild oxen shall be struck down with fat-
  lings,
  and bullocks with bulls;
Their land shall be soaked with blood,
  and their earth greasy with fat.
⁸For the LORD has a day of vengeance,
  a year of requital by Zion's defender.
⁹Edom's streams shall be changed into
  pitch
  and her earth into sulphur,
  and her land shall become burning
  pitch;
¹⁰Night and day it shall not be quenched,

tion of the monarchy and of Zion, which had been major points of reference in the prophecy of Isaiah. Compare the earlier prophecies in Isa 2, 9, and 11.

POSTEXILIC ORACLES

Isa 34:1–35:10

These two chapters are generally believed to belong together. The deliverance of Jerusalem is the counterpart of the destruction of Edom. There are also similarities of language in the two chapters. The setting is after the Exile, when the Jewish community experienced much tension with all its neighbors. Edom lay immediately south of Judah.

34:1-17 Oracle against Edom. This oracle begins with a call to judgment (see Deut 32:1) against all nations and then moves to the specific case of Edom. The presuppositions of the judgment are drawn from the royal ideology: the

its smoke shall rise forever.
From generation to generation she shall
lie waste,
    never again shall anyone pass
through her.
¹¹But the desert owl and hoot owl shall
possess her,
    the screech owl and raven shall dwell
in her.
The LORD will measure her with line and
plummet
    to be an empty waste
    for satyrs to dwell in.
¹²Her nobles shall be no more,
    nor shall kings be proclaimed there;
    all her princes are gone.
¹³Her castles shall be overgrown with
thorns,
    her fortresses with thistles and briers.
She shall become an abode for jackals
    and a haunt for ostriches.
¹⁴Wildcats shall meet with desert beasts,
    satyrs shall call to one another;
There shall the lilith repose,
    and find for herself a place to rest.

¹⁵There the hoot owl shall nest and lay
eggs,
    hatch them out and gather them in
her shadow;
There shall the kites assemble,
    none shall be missing its mate.
¹⁶Look in the book of the LORD and read:
    No one of these shall be lacking,
For the mouth of the LORD has ordered
it,
    and his spirit shall gather them
there.
¹⁷It is he who casts the lot for them,
    and with his hand he marks off their
shares of her;
They shall possess her forever,
    and dwell there from generation to
generation.

Israel's Deliverance

35 ¹The desert and the parched land
will exult;
    the steppe will rejoice and bloom.
²They will bloom with abundant
flowers,

Lord is Zion's defender and defeats all nations that oppose it. The passage is notable for two reasons. First, it uses the imagery of cosmic destruction—the heavens will be rolled up like a scroll. This imagery is obviously metaphorical here. It is a poetic evocation of utter desolation, which attests the absolute power of God over the world. In the later apocalyptic literature this imagery is used in a more literal way.

Second, we cannot overlook the fact that this is a rather gory fantasy of vengeance. It is true that the vengeance of the Lord is closely related to the idea of justice. It is a matter of punishing the oppressor and vindicating the oppressed (see Deut 32:34-43). Yet, it is no less true that this oracle expresses the frustration and resentment of the Jewish community in the hard times of the postexilic period. The sentiments expressed are less than admirable, but they are certainly an honest expression of human nature. Religious people have often expected their God to satisfy their desire for vengeance. The expectation, however, is seldom fulfilled.

35:1-10 A triumphal procession. Chapter 35 provides the positive counterpart to chapter 34 by focusing on Israel's liberation. The imagery is closely related to that of Second Isaiah: there will be a highway in the desert (see Isa 40:3), the desert will bloom and burst forth with springs (see Isa 43:19).

and rejoice with joyful song.
The glory of Lebanon will be given to
them,
the splendor of Carmel and Sharon;
They will see the glory of the LORD,
the splendor of our God.
[3]Strengthen the hands that are feeble,
make firm the knees that are weak,
[4]Say to those whose hearts are
frightened:
Be strong, fear not!
Here is your God,
he comes with vindication;
With divine recompense
he comes to save you.
[5]Then will the eyes of the blind be
opened,
the ears of the deaf be cleared;
[6]Then will the lame leap like a stag,
then the tongue of the dumb will
sing.
Streams will burst forth in the
desert,
and rivers in the steppe.
[7]The burning sands will become pools,

and the thirsty ground, springs of
water;
The abode where jackals lurk
will be a marsh for the reed and
papyrus.
[8]A highway will be there,
called the holy way;
No one unclean may pass over it,
nor fools go astray on it.
[9]No lion will be there,
nor beast of prey go up to be met
upon it.
It is for those with a journey to make,
and on it the redeemed will walk.
[10]Those whom the LORD has ransomed
will return
and enter Zion singing,
crowned with everlasting joy;
They will meet with joy and gladness,
sorrow and mourning will flee.

VII: HISTORICAL APPENDIX

36 Invasion of Sennacherib. [1]In the fourteenth year of King Hezekiah, Sennacherib, king of Assyria,

Verse 10 is repeated directly in Isa 51:11. The liberation involves opening the eyes of the blind and the ears of the deaf (see Isa 42:7). The theme of the procession, which is also fundamental to Second Isaiah, is probably derived from the temple cult. The message is one of comfort and hope. Undoubtedly the author of these chapters saw the destruction of enemies like Edom as a necessary precondition for the transformation. In both cases we must recognize the role of fantasy, but the images of chapter 35 have lasting power to console and encourage those in need of liberation.

STORIES FROM THE TIME OF KING HEZEKIAH

Isa 36:1–39:8

The prose narrative that concludes First Isaiah is paralleled, almost word for word, in 2 Kgs 18:13–20:19. Since the account fits into the ongoing narrative of Kings and is written in the style of that work, we may assume that it was borrowed from there by the editor of Isaiah.

The narrative is made up of three episodes: the invasion of Sennacherib in chapters 36–37, the sickness and recovery of Hezekiah in chapter 38, and

went on an expedition against all the fortified cities of Judah and captured them. ²From Lachish the king of Assyria sent his commander with a great army to King Hezekiah in Jerusalem. When he stopped at the conduit of the upper pool, on the highway of the fuller's field, ³there came out to him the master of the palace, Eliakim, son of Hilkiah, and Shebna the scribe, and the herald Joah, son of Asaph. ⁴The commander said to them, "Tell King Hezekiah: Thus says the great king, the king of Assyria, 'On what do you base this confidence of yours? ⁵Do you think mere words substitute for strategy and might in war? On whom, then, do you rely, that you rebel against me? ⁶This Egypt, the staff on which you rely, is in fact a broken reed which pierces the hand of anyone who leans on it. That is what Pharaoh, king of Egypt, is to all who rely on him. ⁷But if you say to me: "We rely on the LORD, our God," is not he the one whose high places and altars Hezekiah removed, commanding Judah and Jerusalem to worship before this altar?'

⁸"Now, make a wager with my lord the king of Assyria: 'I will give you two thousand horses, if you can put riders on them.' ⁹How then can you repulse even one of the least servants of my lord? And yet you rely on Egypt for chariots and

the Babylonian delegation in chapter 39. The stories in chapters 38 and 39 qualify the miraculous deliverance in chapter 37. Chapter 38 suggests that Hezekiah is a special king in any case, and chapter 39 warns that the deliverance from the Assyrians will not be repeated when the Babylonians attack.

36:1–37:38 The invasion of Sennacherib. The narrative in Isa 36 differs from that of 2 Kgs 18 in one major respect. It omits 2 Kgs 18:14-16, which says that Hezekiah submitted and paid an exorbitant tribute to the king of Assyria, including even the gold overlay from the panels of the temple. The accuracy of that passage in 2 Kings is confirmed by an Assyrian account, which boasts that Hezekiah was shut up in Jerusalem "like a bird in a cage," his territory reduced, some two hundred thousand of his people taken into slavery, and the tribute increased. The account in Isaiah (like 2 Kgs 18:17–19:37) makes no mention of this humiliation but ends instead with a miraculous deliverance by the angel of the Lord.

There are other difficulties in the narrative. 2 Kgs 18:9 puts the accession of Hezekiah before the fall of Samaria, in 725 B.C.E. His fourteenth year then would be 711 B.C.E., but we know that Sennacherib's campaign took place in 701 B.C.E. The dates have been somehow confused in the transmission of the text. Tirhakah, mentioned in Isa 37:9, did not become king of Egypt until 690/89 B.C.E. He is named here by mistake, by an author who evidently wrote long after the events. Moreover, the narrative is not really one account but two—the first in Isa 36:1–37:9a, the second in Isa 37:9b-36. The second account repeats part of the words of the Assyrian messengers from the first account but gives a slightly different account of the role of Isaiah. The main problem, however, concerns the relation of the incident described here to that in 2 Kgs 18:14-16.

horsemen! ¹⁰'Was it without the LORD's will that I have come up to destroy this land? The LORD said to me, "Go up and destroy that land!"'

¹¹Then Eliakim and Shebna and Joah said to the commander, "Please speak to your servants in Aramaic; we understand it. Do not speak to us in Judean within earshot of the people who are on the wall."

¹²But the commander replied, "Was it to you and your master that my lord sent me to speak these words? Was it not rather to the men sitting on the wall, who, with you, will have to eat their own excrement and drink their own urine?"

¹³Then the commander stepped forward and cried out in a loud voice in Judean, "Listen to the words of the great king, the king of Assyria. ¹⁴Thus says the king: 'Do not let Hezekiah deceive you, since he cannot deliver you. ¹⁵Let not Hezekiah induce you to rely on the LORD, saying, 'The LORD will surely save us; this city will not be handed over to the king of Assyria.' ' ¹⁶Do not listen to Hezekiah, for the king of Assyria says: 'Make peace with me and surrender! Then each of you will eat of his own vine and of his own fig tree, and drink the water of his own cistern, ¹⁷until I come to take you to a land like your own, a land of grain and wine, of bread and vineyards. ¹⁸Do not let Hezekiah seduce you by saying, "The LORD will save us." Has any of the gods of the nations ever rescued his land from the hand of the king of Assyria? ¹⁹Where are the gods of Hamath and Arpad? Where are the gods of Sepharvaim? Where are the gods of Samaria? Have they saved Samaria from my hand? ²⁰Which of all the gods of these lands ever

Some scholars resolve this problem (and the mention of Tirhakah) by supposing that there was a second invasion by Sennacherib about 688 B.C.E. There is no extrabiblical evidence for this. It is simpler to suppose that a single invasion was remembered in different ways, as indeed there are differences between the two accounts in Isa 36–37. In that case, we must assume that Hezekiah was forced into submission. The cost to Judah was enormous, but Jerusalem was spared and Hezekiah was allowed to continue on the throne. Even this much must have seemed like a miraculous deliverance to the people of Jerusalem, since they had little hope of withstanding the Assyrian attack.

The reason for Sennacherib's *relative* leniency is not clear. Isa 37:7 suggests that he was eager to return home to forestall conspiracy. Isa 37:9 suggests that he was threatened by an Egyptian advance. There is a report in the Greek historian Herodotus that an Assyrian army was overrun by field mice near the Egyptian border. This report has the appearance of a legend, but some have supposed that it arose from an outbreak of bubonic plague in the Assyrian army, and that this in turn was perceived by the Jews as the work of the angel of the Lord. In any case, Judah had not escaped unscathed. The description of the ravaged land in Isa 1:2-8 probably refers to this time.

36:1–37:9a The first account. The first account is largely taken up with the speech of the Assyrian messengers. The capture of Lachish, southwest

rescued his land from my hand? Will the LORD then save Jerusalem from my hand?' " ²¹But they remained silent and did not answer him one word, for the king had ordered them not to answer him.

²²Then the master of the palace, Eliakim, son of Hilkiah, Shebna the scribe, and the herald Joah, son of Asaph, came to Hezekiah with their garments torn, and reported to him what the commander had said.

37 ¹When King Hezekiah heard this, he tore his garments, wrapped himself in sackcloth, and went into the temple of the LORD. ²He sent Eliakim, the master of the palace, and Shebna the scribe, and the elders of the priests, wrapped in sackcloth, to tell the prophet Isaiah, son of Amoz: ³"Thus says Hezekiah: 'This is a day of distress, of rebuke, and of disgrace. Children are at the point of birth, but there is no strength to bring them forth. ⁴Perhaps the LORD, your

God, will hear the words of the commander, whom his master, the king of Assyria, sent to taunt the living God, and will rebuke him for the words which the LORD, your God, has heard. Send up a prayer for the remnant that is here.' "

⁵When the servants of King Hezekiah had come to Isaiah, ⁶he said to them: "Tell this to your master: 'Thus says the LORD: Do not be frightened by the words you have heard, with which the servants of the king of Assyria have blasphemed me. ⁷I am about to put in him such a spirit that, when he hears a certain report, he will return to his own land, and there I will cause him to fall by the sword.' "

⁸When the commander returned to Lachish and heard that the king of Assyria had left there, he found him besieging Libnah. ⁹The king of Assyria heard a report that Tirhakah, king of Ethiopia, had come out to fight against him. Again

of Jerusalem, is known from an Assyrian wall relief and from excavations at the site. The speech of the messengers is probably a creation of the Jewish author, inspired perhaps by Isaiah's oracle against Assyria in Isa 10:5-11. The unreliability of Egypt might indeed be a theme of Assyrian propaganda, as it was of Isaiah's preaching. The suggestion that Hezekiah had alienated Yahweh by tearing down some altars presupposes knowledge of Hezekiah's reform (2 Chr 29:3–31:21). The claim that Yahweh sent the king of Assyria anticipates the propaganda of Cyrus of Persia at a later time. In all, the speech reads like clever propaganda, although it may tell us more about Jewish perceptions than about Assyrian views. The punch line comes in verse 18: "Has any of the gods of the nations ever rescued his land from the hand of the king of Assyria?" The success of a nation is taken to reflect the power or weakness of its God. In Jewish eyes, the assault on Jerusalem was a direct affront to Yahweh (see Ps 79:10: "Why should the nations say, 'Where is their God?' ").

The response of Isaiah (37:6) in the first account recalls his advice to King Ahaz in Isa 7:4: "Do not fear." The advice to remain calm was not, of course, easy advice in the circumstances, but it was consistent with the prophet's stance throughout his career.

37:9b-36 The second account. The second account elaborates on the role of Isaiah. First, he recites a lengthy psalm, affirming that an attack on Jeru-

he sent envoys to Hezekiah with this message: "Thus shall you say to Hezekiah, king of Judah: [10]Do not let your God on whom you rely deceive you by saying that Jerusalem will not be handed over to the king of Assyria. [11]You yourself have heard what the kings of Assyria have done to all the countries: They doomed them! Will you, then, be saved? [12]Did the gods of the nations whom my fathers destroyed save them? Gozen, Haran, Rezeph, and the Edenites in Telassar? [13]Where is the king of Hamath, the king of Arpad, or a king of the cities of Sepharvaim, Hena or Ivvah?' "

[14]Hezekiah took the letter from the hand of the messengers and read it; then he went up to the temple of the LORD, and spreading it out before him, [15]he prayed to the LORD: [16]"O LORD of hosts, God of Israel, enthroned upon the cherubim! You alone are God over all the kingdoms of the earth. You have made the heavens and the earth. [17]Incline your ear, O LORD, and listen! Open your eyes, O LORD, and see! Hear all the words of the letter that Sennacherib sent to taunt the living God. [18]Truly, O LORD, the kings of Assyria have laid waste all the nations and their lands, [19]and cast their gods into the fire; they destroyed them because they were not gods but the work of human hands, wood and stone. [20]Therefore, O LORD, our God, save us from his hand, that all the kingdoms of the earth may know that you, O LORD, alone are God."

Punishment of Sennacherib. [21]Then Isaiah, son of Amoz, sent this message to Hezekiah: Thus says the LORD, the God of Israel: In answer to your prayer for help against Sennacherib, king of Assyria, [22]this is the word the LORD has spoken concerning him:

She despises you, laughs you to scorn,
  the virgin daughter Zion;
Behind you she wags her head,
  daughter Jerusalem.
[23]Whom have you insulted and blasphemed,
  against whom have you raised your voice
And lifted up your eyes on high?
  Against the Holy One of Israel!
[24]Through your servants you have insulted the Lord:
  You said, "With my many chariots
I climbed the mountain heights,
  the recesses of Lebanon;
I cut down its lofty cedars,
  its choice cypresses;
I reached the remotest heights,
  its forest park.
[25]I dug wells and drank water in foreign lands;

salem is an insult to the Holy One of Israel and is doomed to defeat (see Psalms 2, 48). Some of the wording of the psalm recalls Second Isaiah (37:26; see also 45:21; 46:10), and this contributes to the impression that it does not come from Isaiah himself (also compare 37:29 with Ezek 38:4). In verses 30-32, however, we may well have an authentic prophecy of Isaiah, since it recalls his position in Isa 7. Cultivation will not even be possible for two years. Only a remnant will remain, but it will be the bearer of God's promises to Zion. Here the full cost to Judah is acknowledged.

Isaiah's prophecy of the remnant is overlaid here, however, with pious legend. First, in verses 33-35 Isaiah is said to prophesy that the Assyrians would not even reach Jerusalem. The Assyrian account, by contrast, explicitly claims to have cast up earthworks against the city. Then comes the action of the angel of the Lord. Even if we assume that a large number of Assyrians

I dried up with the soles of my feet
all the rivers of Egypt.
²⁶Have you not heard?
Long ago I prepared it,
From days of old I planned it,
now I have brought it to pass:
That you should reduce fortified cities
into heaps of ruins,
²⁷While their inhabitants, shorn of power,
are dismayed and ashamed,
Becoming like the plants of the field,
like the green growth,
like the scorched grass on the housetops.
²⁸I am aware whether you stand or sit;
I know whether you come or go,
and also your rage against me.
²⁹Because of your rage against me
and your fury which has reached
my ears,
I will put my hook in your nose
and my bit in your mouth,
and make you return the way you
came.
³⁰This shall be a sign for you:
this year you shall eat the after-
growth,
next year, what grows of itself;
But in the third year, sow and reap,
plant vineyards and eat their fruit!
³¹The remaining survivors of the house
of Judah

shall again strike root below
and bear fruit above.
³²For out of Jerusalem shall come a
remnant,
and from Mount Zion, survivors.
The zeal of the LORD of hosts shall do
this.

³³Therefore, thus says the LORD concerning the king of Assyria: He shall not
reach this city, nor shoot an arrow at it,
nor come before it with a shield, nor cast
up siegeworks against it. ³⁴He shall return
by the same way he came, without enter-
ing the city, says the LORD. ³⁵I will shield
and save this city for my own sake, and
for the sake of my servant David.

³⁶The angel of the LORD went forth and
struck down one hundred and eighty-five
thousand in the Assyrian camp. Early the
next morning, there they were, all the
corpses of the dead. ³⁷So Sennacherib, the
king of Assyria, broke camp and went
back home to Nineveh.

³⁸When he was worshiping in the
temple of his god Nisroch, his sons
Adrammelech and Sharezer slew him
with the sword and fled into the land of
Ararat. His son Esarhaddon reigned in his
stead.

38 Sickness and Recovery of Heze-
kiah. ¹In those days, when He-

died in a plague (185,000 is impossibly high), attribution of this to the angel
of the Lord requires a leap of faith and is the stuff of legend.

What actually happened is far from clear. Sennacherib must have offered
Hezekiah terms that did not require his abdication, and he accepted. Whether
Isaiah approved of the surrender is not reported. The occasion can hardly
have aroused much rejoicing in Jerusalem. Yet, with the passage of time the
humiliation was forgotten, and the fact that Jerusalem was not destroyed
was seen as proof of God's protection. In one sense this showed a proper
appreciation of the gift of life, which was preserved against all expectations.
On the other hand, it surely contributed to the complacent belief that Zion
could never fall, a belief that Jeremiah encountered with much frustration
a century later.

The violent death of Sennacherib is also reported in nonbiblical stories.

zekiah was mortally ill, the prophet Isaiah, son of Amoz, came and said to him: "Thus says the LORD: Put your house in order, for you are about to die; you shall not recover." ²Then Hezekiah turned his face to the wall and prayed to the LORD:

³"O LORD, remember how faithfully and wholeheartedly I conducted myself in your presence, doing what was pleasing to you!" And Hezekiah wept bitterly.

⁴Then the word of the LORD came to Isaiah: ⁵"Go, tell Hezekiah: Thus says the LORD, the God of your father David: I have heard your prayer and seen your tears. I will heal you: in three days you shall go up to the LORD's temple; I will add fifteen years to your life. ⁶I will rescue you and this city from the hand of the king of Assyria; I will be a shield to this city."

²¹Isaiah then ordered a poultice of figs to be taken and applied to the boil, that he might recover. ²²Then Hezekiah asked, "What is the sign that I shall go up to the temple of the LORD?"

⁷[Isaiah answered:] "This will be the sign for you from the LORD that he will do what he has promised: ⁸See, I will make the shadow cast by the sun on the stairway to the terrace of Ahaz go back the ten steps it has advanced." So the sun came back the ten steps it had advanced.

Hezekiah's Hymn of Thanksgiving. ⁹The song of Hezekiah, king of Judah, after he had been sick and had recovered from his illness:

¹⁰Once I said,
 "In the noontime of life I must depart!
To the gates of the nether world I shall be consigned
 for the rest of my years."
¹¹I said, "I shall see the LORD no more
 in the land of the living.
No longer shall I behold my fellow men
 among those who dwell in the world."
¹²My dwelling, like a shepherd's tent,
 is struck down and borne away from me;
You have folded up my life, like a weaver
 who severs the last thread.
Day and night you give me over to torment;
¹³ I cry out until the dawn.
Like a lion he breaks all my bones;
 [day and night you give me over to torment].
¹⁴Like a swallow I utter shrill cries;
 I moan like a dove.
My eyes grow weak, gazing heavenward:
 O LORD, I am in straits; be my surety!
¹⁵What am I to say or tell him?
 He has done it!
I shall go on through all my years
 despite the bitterness of my soul.
¹⁶Those live whom the LORD protects;

38:1-8 The sickness of Hezekiah. The king's own experience parallels the deliverance of Jerusalem. At first his death seems certain; then he gets a reprieve. The reason is apparently his wholehearted piety. We may infer that this is also why Jerusalem was reprieved. Things might be different under another king. This story, too, has a legendary quality in the supernatural sign of the reversal of the sun. Such stories are meant to arouse wonder, not to report fact. Note that Hezekiah is not criticized for asking for a sign, as Ahaz had been.

38:9-20 Hymn of thanksgiving. Hezekiah recites a psalm of a type that is well-attested in the Psalter (see Psalms 6, 13, 22). It begins by describing the plaintiff's distress and then moves to thanksgiving for the Lord's deliver-

yours . . . the life of my spirit.
You have given me health and life;
¹⁷ thus is my bitterness transformed
into peace.
You have preserved my life
from the pit of destruction,
When you cast behind your back
all my sins.
¹⁸For it is not the nether world that gives
you thanks,
nor death that praises you;
Neither do those who go down into the
pit
await your kindness.
¹⁹The living, the living give you thanks,
as I do today.
Fathers declare to their sons,
O God, your faithfulness.
²⁰The Lord is our savior;
we shall sing to stringed instruments
In the house of the Lord
all the days of our life.

39 Embassy from Merodach-baladan. ¹At that time when
Merodach-baladan, son of Baladan, king
of Babylon, heard that Hezekiah had recovered from his sickness, he sent letters

and gifts to him. ²Hezekiah was pleased
at this, and therefore showed the messengers his treasury, the silver and gold,
the spices and fine oil, his whole armory,
and everything that was in his storerooms; there was nothing in his house or
in his whole realm that he did not show
them.

³Then Isaiah the prophet came to King
Hezekiah and asked him, "What did these
men say to you? Where did they come
from?" Hezekiah answered, "They came
to me from a distant land, from Babylon." ⁴"What did they see in your house?"
he asked. Hezekiah replied, "They saw
everything in my house; there is nothing
in my storerooms that I did not show
them."

⁵Then Isaiah said to Hezekiah, "Hear
the word of the Lord of hosts: ⁶Behold,
the days shall come when all that is in
your house, and everything that your
fathers have stored up until this day, shall
be carried off to Babylon; nothing shall
be left, says the Lord. ⁷Some of your own
bodily descendants shall be taken and
made servants in the palace of the king

ance. The moral in 38:16 applies also to the experience of Jerusalem in the
preceding chapter. Note that this psalm entertains no hope for God's favor
beyond death. The finality of death made the plight of Hezekiah and of Jerusalem all the more urgent.

39:1-8 The delegation from Babylon. The story of the delegation from
Babylon prepares us for the transition to the Babylonian era. The fall of Jerusalem to the Babylonians is never described in the Book of Isaiah, but it is
the presupposition of Isa 40–55. The editor of the book fills the gap by hav-
ing Isaiah prophesy it here in the story taken from 2 Kgs 20. At the same
time, the prophecy corrects the impression that Zion cannot fall, which might
be derived from chapters 36–37.

Hezekiah's action in displaying his treasures is typical of ancient diplomacy
and was designed to impress his visitors. Babylon at that time was a rising
power eager to foster rebellion against Assyria. That such a delegation should
have visited Hezekiah is not in itself implausible. Hezekiah's reaction to
Isaiah's prediction smacks of Louis XIV's famous dictum *"Après moi le
déluge."* The author probably meant only to emphasize that Hezekiah ended

of Babylon." [8]Hezekiah replied to Isaiah, "The word of the LORD which you have spoken is favorable." For he thought, "There will be peace and security in my lifetime."

B. THE BOOK OF CONSOLATION
I: THE LORD'S GLORY IN ISRAEL'S LIBERATION
Promise of Salvation

40 [1]Comfort, give comfort to my people,
says your God.
[2]Speak tenderly to Jerusalem, and proclaim to her
that her service is at an end,
her guilt is expiated;
Indeed, she has received from the hand
of the LORD
double for all her sins.
[3]   A voice cries out:
In the desert prepare the way of the
LORD!
Make straight in the wasteland a
highway for our God!
[4]Every valley shall be filled in,
every mountain and hill shall be made
low;

his days in peace because of his piety. (Compare the idea that the punishment of King Ahaz was deferred until the time of his son because he repented [1 Kgs 21:29].)

SECOND ISAIAH
Isa 40-55

At Isa 40:1 we move to a new setting at the end of the Babylonian Exile (539 B.C.E.), and the oracles that follow are very different from those of Isa 1–39 in tone. They are often called the "Book of Consolation." Unlike chapters 1–39, all the oracles in these chapters are likely to be the work of a single prophet. They may be divided into two parts: chapters 40–48 deal predominantly with liberation from Babylon; chapters 49–55 with the restoration of Zion. The difference between these parts, however, is a matter of degree of emphasis and cannot be taken to indicate different origins or settings.

LIBERATION FROM BABYLON
Isa 40:1–48:22

The first part of Second Isaiah takes the good news that the Exile is at an end as the occasion to contrast Israel and Babylon and their respective gods.

40:1-11 The proclamation of release. This passage serves as an introduction to all of Second Isaiah by specifying the occasion of the oracles—the release of Israel from the Babylonian Exile. In Ezra 1 this event is attributed to a decree of Cyrus, king of Persia. The prophet, however, claims that there

The rugged land shall be made a plain,
   the rough country, a broad valley.
⁵Then the glory of the LORD shall be revealed,
   and all mankind shall see it together;
   for the mouth of the LORD has spoken.
⁶A voice says, "Cry out!"
   I answer, "What shall I cry out?"
"All mankind is grass,
   and all their glory like the flower of the field.
⁷The grass withers, the flower wilts,
   when the breath of the LORD blows upon it.
   [So then, the people is the grass.]
⁸Though the grass withers and the flower wilts,
   the word of our God stands forever."
⁹Go up onto a high mountain,
   Zion, herald of glad tidings;
Cry out at the top of your voice,
   Jerusalem, herald of good news!
Fear not to cry out
   and say to the cities of Judah:
   Here is your God!
¹⁰Here comes with power

is a more fundamental cause, namely, a decree of Yahweh in the heavenly council. The idea of a heavenly council of gods was widespread in the ancient world and was based on the assumption that God has a royal court like any great king. Vivid biblical illustrations are found in Psalm 82, 1 Kgs 22, and Isa 6. The scene in Isa 40 may be viewed as a counterpoint to that of Isa 6. In the earlier chapter the decree was one of judgment on Israel; here it is one of consolation. (Note that Jerusalem can stand for the people as a whole.)

Verse 2 presupposes the usual view that the Exile was a punishment for Israel's sins, but adds that Israel has received "double for all her sins." The implication is that the suffering is not fully explained as punishment. We will find later that Second Isaiah finds a more positive way to understand the experience of the Exile.

The voice in verse 3 is the voice of an angel implementing the divine decree. The "way" is analogous to the great ritual processions of the Babylonian gods, but also the triumphal procession of Yahweh from Mount Sinai at the time of the Exodus (compare Ps 68:8-9; Deut 33:3). The Exodus motif is made explicit by the location "in the desert." The return from Babylon is seen as a reenactment of the original liberation of Israel out of Egypt. The hope for a new Exodus was found as early as Hosea (ch. 2) in the eighth century, but now Second Isaiah claims that it is actually taking place.

The liberation of Israel is viewed as a revelation of God. In the first Exodus, Israel's God went before the people in a pillar of cloud or a pillar of fire. Now all flesh would see the glory of God. The prophet is told to proclaim the difference between the passing power of humanity and the unshakable word of God. The power of the Babylonians, which had seemed so great, had now faded like the grass of the field.

In verses 9-11 Zion/Jerusalem is told to proclaim the good news to "the cities of Judah." (The familiar translation "O thou who bringest good tid-

the Lord God,
who rules by his strong arm;
Here is his reward with him,
his recompense before him.

[11]Like a shepherd he feeds his flock;
in his arms he gathers the lambs,
Carrying them in his bosom,
and leading the ewes with care.

Power of the Creator To Save His People

[12]Who has cupped in his hand the waters
of the sea,
and marked off the heavens with a
span?
Who has held in a measure the dust of
the earth,
weighed the mountains in scales
and the hills in a balance?

[13]Who has directed the spirit of the Lord,
or has instructed him as his counselor?

[14]Whom did he consult to gain knowledge?
Who taught him the path of judgment,
or showed him the way of understanding?

[15]Behold, the nations count as a drop of
the bucket,
as dust on the scales;
the coastlands weigh no more than
powder.

[16]Lebanon would not suffice for fuel,
nor its animals be enough for
holocausts.

[17]Before him all the nations are as nought,
as nothing and void he accounts
them.

[18]To whom can you liken God?
With what equal can you confront
him?

[19]An idol, cast by a craftsman,

ings to Zion" is possible but improbable, since the verbs are feminine in agreement with Zion.) Here again Jerusalem is an ideal figure, representing the
community of exiles who would join the prophet in returning to restore the
actual city. We should bear in mind that not all the Jews who were in Babylon took the opportunity to return; many decided that they were better off
in exile. The prophet is not only proclaiming deliverance but urging the people
to accept it. He bases his exhortation on the assurance that God is with
them with power, but also with loving care, suggested by the popular image
of the shepherd (compare Psalm 23 and John 10).

This passage of Second Isaiah is best known to Christian readers from
the citations in Matt 3:3 and John 1:23, where Isa 40:3 is taken to mean "the
voice of one crying in the wilderness" and applied to John the Baptist. The
citation is not quite accurate and does not give the original meaning of the
passage. The application to John was apt enough, however, since he too was
proclaiming a new act of salvation like the Exodus, and he set himself to
prepare for it.

40:12-31 The incomparable God. The threefold oracle in verses 12-31
follows naturally from the declaration "Here is your God" in verse 9. The
first stanza (vv. 12-17) asks a series of rhetorical questions reminiscent of
Job 38–41. The implied answer is that it is Yahweh alone who has created
the earth. The nations are as nothing before Yahweh, since the whole earth
is in this God's grasp.

which the smith plates with gold
and fits with silver chains?
²⁰Mulberry wood, the choice portion
which a skilled craftsman picks out
for himself,
Choosing timber that will not rot,
to set up an idol that will not be
unsteady?
⁴¹⁶One man helps another,
one says to the other, "Keep on!"
⁴¹⁷The craftsman encourages the goldsmith,
the one who beats with the hammer,
him who strikes on the anvil;
He says the soldering is good,
and he fastens it with nails to steady
it.
²¹Do you not know? Have you not
heard?
Was it not foretold you from the beginning?
Have you not understood? Since the
earth was founded
²²He sits enthroned above the vault of the
earth,
and its inhabitants are like grass-
hoppers;

He stretches out the heavens like a veil,
spreads them out like a tent to dwell
in.
²³He brings princes to nought
and makes the rulers of the earth as
nothing.
²⁴Scarcely are they planted or sown,
scarcely is their stem rooted in the
earth,
When he breathes upon them and they
wither,
and the stormwind carries them away
like straw.
²⁵To whom can you liken me as an equal?
says the Holy One.
²⁶Lift up your eyes on high
and see who has created these:
He leads out their army and numbers
them,
calling them all by name.

By his great might and the strength of
his power
not one of them is missing!
²⁷Why, O Jacob, do you say,
and declare, O Israel,
"My way is hidden from the LORD,

The second stanza (vv. 18-24) begins with another rhetorical question: To whom can God be likened? Second Isaiah mocks the statue-makers, as he will do at much greater length in chapter 44. (The New American Bible unnecessarily inserts verses 6-7 of chapter 41 here.) The initial question is balanced by another: "Do you not know? Have you not heard?" (40:21). What has been told from the beginning is the sovereign power of Yahweh to bring princes to nought and make rulers as nothing (40:23; compare Psalm 107). Yahweh's ability to overthrow the Babylonians comes from the fact that it was Yahweh who created the earth, as the cult tradition of Jerusalem had long claimed (for example, Psalms 93, 95).

The third stanza (vv. 25-31) closely parallels the second in form. The introductory question, "To whom can you liken me . . . ?" (40:25), is followed by a command to look up at the stars, which were often honored as divine by Babylonians. The prophet shares the common belief that the stars are a heavenly host of supernatural beings but insists that they are subject to Yahweh, who keeps them in order. At this point the prophet directly reproaches the Israelites for their despair in feeling abandoned by their God.

and my right is disregarded by my God"?

⁸Do you not know
or have you not heard?
The LORD is the eternal God,
creator of the ends of the earth.
He does not faint nor grow weary,
and his knowledge is beyond scrutiny.
²⁹He gives strength to the fainting;
for the weak he makes vigor abound.
³⁰Though young men faint and grow weary,
and youths stagger and fall,
³¹They that hope in the LORD will renew their strength,
they will soar as with eagles' wings;
They will run and not grow weary,
walk and not grow faint.

The Liberator of Israel

41 ¹Keep silence before me, O coastlands;
you peoples, wait for my words!

Let them draw near and speak;
let us come together for judgment.
²Who has stirred up from the East the champion of justice,
and summoned him to be his attendant?
To him he delivers the nations
and subdues the kings;
With his sword he reduces them to dust,
with his bow, to driven straw.
³He pursues them, passing on without loss,
by a path his feet do not even tread.
⁴Who has performed these deeds?
He who has called forth the generations since the beginning.
I, the LORD, am the first,
and with the last I will also be.
⁵The coastlands see, and fear;
the ends of the earth tremble:
these things are near, they come to pass.
⁸But you, Israel, my servant,
Jacob, whom I have chosen,
offspring of Abraham and friend—

The second half of the stanza, "Do you not know, or have you not heard?" (40:28), responds directly to this despair. The Creator is everlasting. Not only does God not grow faint but the Creator is a source of renewed power for those who are attentive to the divine will. Hope did not come easily to the Jews during the Exile. It was only possible for those who deeply believed that their God was indeed the supreme God. Second Isaiah was convinced that his faith was now vindicated by the fall of Babylon. Note that in verse 25 God is called "the Holy One," a title often found in First Isaiah.

41:1–42:9 Judgment and election. Many commentators divide this long passage into several short oracles. In particular, 42:1-4 is commonly set apart as one of the so-called "Servant Songs." The key to understanding the passage, however, is to recognize that there are two parallel and complementary trial scenes in 41:1-20 and 41:21–42:9. In each case there is:

summons to trial	41:1	41:21
legal questioning	41:2-4	41:22-29
election and reassurance of Israel	41:5-20	42:1-9

In the first scene the nations are summoned for judgment. The issue to be decided is: Who raised up Cyrus of Persia, the "champion of justice,"

⁹You whom I have taken from the ends
   of the earth
   and summoned from its far-off
      places,
You whom I have called my servant,
   whom I have chosen and will not cast
      off—
¹⁰Fear not, I am with you;
   be not dismayed; I am your God.
I will strengthen you, and help you,
   and uphold you with my right hand
      of justice.
¹¹Yes, all shall be put to shame and dis-
      grace
   who vent their anger against you;
Those shall perish and come to nought
   who offer resistance.
¹²You shall seek out, but shall not find,
   those who strive against you;
They shall be as nothing at all
   who do battle with you.
¹³For I am the LORD, your God,
   who grasp your right hand;
It is I who say to you, "Fear not,
   I will help you."
¹⁴Fear not, O worm Jacob,
   O maggot Israel;
I will help you, says the LORD;
   your redeemer is the Holy One of
      Israel.
¹⁵I will make of you a threshing sledge,
   sharp, new, and double-edged,
To thresh the mountains and crush
      them,
   to make the hills like chaff.
¹⁶When you winnow them, the wind shall

carry them off
   and the storm shall scatter them.
But you shall rejoice in the LORD,
   and glory in the Holy One of Israel.
¹⁷The afflicted and the needy seek water in
      vain,
   their tongues are parched with thirst.
I, the LORD, will answer them;
   I, the God of Israel, will not forsake
      them.
¹⁸I will open up rivers on the bare
      heights,
   and fountains in the broad valleys;
I will turn the desert into a marshland,
   and the dry ground into springs of
      water.
¹⁹I will plant in the desert the cedar,
   acacia, myrtle, and olive;
I will set in the wasteland the cypress,
   together with the plane tree and the
      pine,
²⁰That all may see and know,
   observe and understand,
That the hand of the LORD has done this,
   the Holy One of Israel has created it.
²¹Present your case, says the LORD;
   bring forward your reasons, says the
      King of Jacob.
²²Let them come near and foretell to us
   what it is that shall happen!
What are the things of long ago?
   Tell us, that we may reflect on them
And know their outcome;
   or declare to us the things to come!
²³Foretell the things that shall come
      afterward,

who overthrew Babylon? The answer is given unequivocally: Yahweh, first and last, is responsible for all developments in history. Verses 5-7 (verses 6-7 are inserted after 40:20 in our text) parody the reaction of the Gentiles. They have to encourage one another in making their idols, since the idols cannot encourage them. By contrast, Israel is chosen as the Servant of the Lord. However despised Israel may be in the Exile as a "worm" or "maggot" (compare Ps 22:6), there is no reason to fear. Yahweh is the servant's redeemer (41:14), buying his freedom from slavery. This section concludes with a prophecy of the transformation of the desert with water for the needy. The reference to the desert suggests that the Exodus theme is implied here and

that we may know that you are gods!
Do something, good or evil,
    that will put us in awe and in fear.
²⁴Why, you are nothing and your work is
        nought!
    To choose you is an abomination.

⁵I have stirred up one from the north,
        and he comes;
    from the east I summon him by name;
He shall trample the rulers down like red
        earth,
    as the potter treads the clay.
⁶Who announced this from the begin-
        ning, that we might know;
    beforehand, that we might say it is
        true?
Not one of you foretold it, not one
        spoke;
    no one heard you say,

²⁷"The first news for Zion: they are com-
        ing now,"
    or, "For Jerusalem I will pick out a
        bearer of the glad tidings."
²⁸When I look, there is not one,
    no one of them to give counsel,
    to make an answer when I question
        them.
²⁹Ah, all of them are nothing,
    their works are nought,
    their idols are empty wind!

The Servant of the Lord

42 ¹Here is my servant whom I up-
        hold,
    my chosen one with whom I am
        pleased,
Upon whom I have put my spirit;
    he shall bring forth justice to the
        nations,

that the poor and needy are Israel. The transformation, however, is also for the Gentiles, so that they will recognize the work of the Holy One of Israel.

The second section has a long series of questions and constitutes a more coherent trial. The challenge is: Which of the gods had foretold the rise of Cyrus, and, more crucially, had heralded good news for Israel? The answer is a resounding "Not one." The conclusion is that "all of them are nothing" (41:29). Second Isaiah is more emphatic in denying the power of pagan gods than any earlier biblical book. The argument presupposes the prophet's faith that it is Yahweh who is responsible for the surprising collapse of the power of Babylon. Anyone who did not already share that faith would hardly be persuaded.

The so-called Servant Song in 42:1-4 corresponds to 41:8-9 in singling out a chosen Servant. In both passages the Servant is Israel, conceived in terms of its ideal destiny. The mission of the Servant is specified much more fully in chapter 42 than in chapter 41. The spirit of the Lord is upon him, as on the messianic king in Isa 11. He is to bring justice to the nations, but in a nonviolent, nonaggressive way. The role is further elaborated in 42:6-7. The Servant is a covenant of the people, a light to the nations. We may recall the portrayal of Mount Zion as a center for the nations in Isa 2:2-4. The precise understanding of "a covenant of the people" (42:6) is disputed, but the idea seems to be that God makes a covenant with the nations through the mediation of Israel. The Servant is also sent to open the eyes of the blind and liberate the imprisoned. In the following passages the "blind" refers to

²Not crying out, not shouting,
  not making his voice heard in the
    street.
³A bruised reed he shall not break,
  and a smoldering wick he shall not
    quench,
⁴Until he establishes justice on the earth;
  the coastlands will wait for his teach-
    ing.
⁵Thus says God, the Lord,
  who created the heavens and
    stretched them out,
  who spreads out the earth with its
    crops,
Who gives breath to its people
  and spirit to those who walk on it:
⁶I, the Lord, have called you for the vic-
    tory of justice,
  I have grasped you by the hand;
I formed you, and set you
  as a covenant of the people,
  a light for the nations,
⁷To open the eyes of the blind,
  to bring out prisoners from confine-
    ment,
  and from the dungeon, those who live
    in darkness.

⁸I am the Lord, this is my name;
  my glory I give to no other,
  nor my praise to idols.
⁹See, the earlier things have come to
    pass,
  new ones I now foretell;
Before they spring into being,
  I announce them to you.

The Salvation of Israel despite Its Sins

¹⁰Sing to the Lord a new song,
  his praise from the end of the earth:
Let the sea and what fills it resound,
  the coastlands, and those who dwell
    in them.
¹¹Let the steppe and its cities cry out,
  the villages where Kedar dwells;
Let the inhabitants of Sela exult,
  and shout from the top of the moun-
    tains.
¹²Let them give glory to the Lord,
  and utter his praise in the coastlands.
¹³The Lord goes forth like a hero,
  like a warrior he stirs up his ardor;
He shouts out his battle cry,
  against his enemies he shows his
    might:

Israel (42:16) and specifically to the Servant in 42:19! The most obvious "prisoners" in this context are the Jewish exiles in Babylon. Yet, the Servant Israel is being sent to help the blind and imprisoned.

Some scholars have drawn the conclusion that the Servant in this passage is not Israel but an individual, and that the passage comes from a different hand than the surrounding oracles. We will see in Isa 42:18–43:8, however, that there is considerable ambiguity in the idea of the Servant. There is tension between the ideal of what Israel is supposed to be and what the community actually is. It is Israel's destiny to be a light to the nations, but in order to fulfill this, the blind among the people must recover their sight and the exiles must be liberated.

The section concludes with affirmations that God does not give divine glory to idols (compare 41:6-7) and that "the earlier things have come to pass" (42:9; compare 41:22-23, 26). In this way the prophet concludes this long section by referring back to two important themes of chapter 41.

42:10-17 A hymn to Yahweh the warrior. The "new song" (v. 10) is a hymn of praise like Psalms 96 and 98, which begin with the same invita-

¹⁴I have looked away, and kept silence,
  I have said nothing, holding myself
    in;
But now, I cry out as a woman in labor,
  gasping and panting.
¹⁵I will lay waste mountains and hills,
  all their herbage I will dry up;
I will turn the rivers into marshes,
  and the marshes I will dry up.
¹⁶I will lead the blind on their journey;
  by paths unknown I will guide them.
I will turn darkness into light before
    them,
  and make crooked ways straight.
These things I do for them,
  and I will not forsake them.

¹⁷They shall be turned back in utter shame
  who trust in idols;
Who say to molten images,
  "You are our gods."
¹⁸You who are deaf, listen,
  you who are blind, look and see!
¹⁹Who is blind but my servant,
  or deaf like the messenger I send?

²⁰You see many things without taking
    note;
  your ears are open, but without hear-
    ing.
²¹Though it pleased the LORD in his justice
  to make his law great and glorious,

²²This is a people despoiled and plun-
    dered,
  all of them trapped in holes,
  hidden away in prisons.
They are taken as booty, with no one
    to rescue them,
  as spoil, with no one to demand their
    return.
²³Who of you gives ear to this?
  Who listens and pays heed for the
    time to come?
²⁴Who was it that gave Jacob to be plun-
    dered,
  Israel to the despoilers?
Was it not the LORD, against whom we
    have sinned?
In his ways they refused to walk,
  his law they disobeyed.
²⁵So he poured out wrath upon them,
  his anger, and the fury of battle;
It blazed round about them, yet they did
    not realize,
  it burned them, but they took it not
    to heart.

Promises of Redemption and Restoration

43 ¹But now, thus says the LORD,
  who created you, O Jacob,
and formed you, O Israel:
Fear not, for I have redeemed you;

tion. The reason for praise is given in verses 13-17: Yahweh the warrior, who has held back for a time, will let loose divine anger. Here again there is reference to the Exodus, when Yahweh was first recognized as a warrior (Exod 15:3). The divine warrior was traditionally supposed to have a destructive effect on nature (Isa 42:15; compare Judg 5:4-5; Hab 3:5-15; Nah 1:2-6). In Exodus 15 God leads the people to their triumphant occupation of the land; here too God will lead the "blind" Jews on their return journey. The confusion of idol worshipers in verse 17 is the corollary of the recognition of Yahweh as the true God.

42:18–43:8 The deaf and the blind. Despite his general euphoria, the prophet has moments of dejection. The address to his people as "blind and deaf" betrays some frustration on his part. The problem is not only that they are despoiled and plundered but they have become indifferent. So the prophet insists that even their humiliation in the Exile was the work of their God

I have called you by name: you are mine.

²When you pass through the water, I will be with you;
in the rivers you shall not drown.
When you walk through fire, you shall not be burned;
the flames shall not consume you.
³For I am the LORD, your God,
the Holy One of Israel, your savior.
I give Egypt as your ransom,
Ethiopia and Seba in return for you.
⁴Because you are precious in my eyes
and glorious, and because I love you.
I give men in return for you
and peoples in exchange for your life.
⁵Fear not, for I am with you;
from the east I will bring back your descendants,
from the west I will gather you.
⁶I will say to the north: Give them up!
and to the south: Hold not back!
Bring back my sons from afar,
and my daughters from the ends of the earth:

⁷Everyone who is named as mine,
whom I created for my glory,
whom I formed and made.
⁸Lead out the people who are blind
though they have eyes,
who are deaf though they have ears.
⁹Let all the nations gather together,
let the peoples assemble!
Who among them could have revealed this,
or foretold to us the earlier things?
Let them produce witnesses to prove themselves right,
that one may hear and say, "It is true!"
¹⁰You are my witnesses, says the LORD,
my servants whom I have chosen
To know and believe in me
and understand that it is I.
Before me no god was formed,
and after me there shall be none.
¹¹It is I, I the LORD;
there is no savior but me.
¹²It is I who foretold, I who saved;
I made it known, not any strange god

and was a punishment for sin. Yet Israel is still the Servant (42:19). The tension between Israel's vocation as Servant and its present reality is most obvious in this passage. Despite the past divine wrath, God has now redeemed Israel and promises to protect it in any ordeal, be it fire or water. The Holy One is identified as the savior of Israel, which is more precious than Egypt or Ethiopia. The implication is that the Persians will be allowed to conquer other countries in return for the release of Israel. The reason given in 43:4 is simply "because I love you" (compare Deut 9, which insists that the original gift of the land was not merited by Israel). The new Exodus is an Exodus of the blind.

There is some vacillation in Second Isaiah's portrayal of Israel. Some passages emphasize the ideal, what Israel is called to be, and minimize the people's sin. This passage is exceptional in its frank criticism of their shortcomings. The apparent inconsistency comes not only from the emotional intensity of the prophet but also from the nature of his program, which was to project an ideal of Yahweh's Servant that was not fully realized in the exilic community.

43:9-12 The Servant as witness. This brief trial scene repeats some of the motifs of the longer unit in 41:1–42:9. Again the issue is who is the true

among you;
You are my witnesses, says the LORD.
I am God, ¹³yes, from eternity I am
He;
There is none who can deliver from my
hand:
who can countermand what I do?
¹⁴Thus says the LORD, your redeemer,
the Holy One of Israel:
For your sakes I send to Babylon;
I will lower all the bars,
and the Chaldeans shall cry out in
lamentation.
¹⁵I am the LORD, your Holy One,
the creator of Israel, your King.
¹⁶Thus says the LORD,
who opens a way in the sea
and a path in the mighty waters,
¹⁷Who leads out chariots and horsemen,
a powerful army,
Till they lie prostrate together, never to
rise,
snuffed out and quenched like a wick.
¹⁸Remember not the events of the past,
the things of long ago consider not;
¹⁹See, I am doing something new!

Now it springs forth, do you not
perceive it?
In the desert I make a way,
in the wasteland, rivers.
²⁰Wild beasts honor me,
jackals and ostriches,
For I put water in the desert
and rivers in the wasteland
for my chosen people to drink,
²¹The people whom I formed for myself,
that they might announce my praise.
²²Yet you did not call upon me, O Jacob,
for you grew weary of me, O Israel.
²³You did not bring me sheep for your
holocausts,
nor honor me with your sacrifices.
I did not exact from you the service of
offerings,
nor weary you for frankincense.
²⁴You did not buy me sweet cane for
money,
nor fill me with the fat of your sacrifices;
Instead, you burdened me with your
sins,
and wearied me with your crimes.

God, and the test is the ability to foretell the future. A new motif is introduced with the idea that the Jewish people are witnesses. They are called "my servant" collectively (the Hebrew reads the singular; the New American Bible changes it to "my servants"). The mission of witnessing is the same as being "a light for the nations" (42:6). Whereas in earlier times the Davidic king was Yahweh's representative on earth, that role has now passed to the people.

Isa 43:10 is exceptionally strong in its denial of the other gods and may be taken to mean that they do not even exist. The prophet is not a philosopher, however. What concerns him is not the existence of the gods as such but the power to save. He is completely unequivocal in his assertion that there is no savior but Yahweh.

43:14–44:5 Exodus and election. The immediate point of reference in this oracle is stated at the outset: the release of the Jews from Babylon. Isa 43:15-21 puts this event in context. Yahweh is the creator of Israel by virtue of the Exodus, yet the Jews are told not to remember the things of the past. The Exodus is not past history! It is something new, something that is happening in the present. The present tense in verse 16 ("opening a way . . .") is quite deliberate. God's saving action, summed up in the Exodus story, is

²⁵It is I, I, who wipe out,
   for my own sake, your offenses;
   your sins I remember no more.
²⁶Would you have me remember, have us
      come to trial?
   Speak up, prove your innocence!
²⁷Your first father sinned;
   your spokesmen rebelled against me
²⁸Till I repudiated the holy gates,
   put Jacob under the ban,
   and exposed Israel to scorn.

44 ¹Hear then, O Jacob, my servant,
      Israel, whom I have chosen.
²Thus says the LORD who made you,
   your help, who formed you from the
      womb:
Fear not, O Jacob, my servant,
   the darling whom I have chosen.
³I will pour out water upon the thirsty
      ground,
   and streams upon the dry land;
I will pour out my spirit upon your
      offspring,
   and my blessing upon your descend-
      ants.
⁴They shall spring up amid the verdure

like poplars beside the flowing
   waters.
⁵One shall say, "I am the LORD's,"
   another shall be named after Jacob,
And this one shall write on his hand,
   "The LORD's,"
   and Israel shall be his surname.

The True God and False Gods

⁶Thus says the LORD, Israel's King
   and redeemer, the LORD of hosts:
I am the first and I am the last;
   there is no God but me.
⁷Who is like me? Let him stand up and
      speak,
   make it evident, and confront me
      with it.
Who of old announced future events?
   Let them foretell to us the things to
      come.
⁸Fear not, be not troubled:
   did I not announce and foretell it long
      ago?
You are my witnesses! Is there a God
   or any Rock besides me?
⁹Idol makers all amount to nothing, and

not all past but is repeatable. Exodus is a pattern in history. What matters is not so much whether it happened in the time of Moses but whether it is happening in the present. Second Isaiah thus points the ways to using the Exodus story to throw light on a new situation. In our own time the Exodus story has been appropriated in a similar way by the liberation theologians of Latin America.

The original Exodus was followed by failure on Israel's part (see espe-cially the indictment in Deut 32). Second Isaiah acknowledges this and even asserts that the destruction of Jerusalem was a punishment for Israel's sin. (The "first father" in 43:27 is probably Jacob; compare Hos 12:3.) Yet Jacob is also the Servant, formed from the womb (44:2; compare 49:5). The descen-dants of Israel will fulfill their destiny by the help of the spirit (compare 42:1), which will vitalize them as water brings life to dry ground. Compare the transforming power of the spirit in Ezek 36, where there is also an analogy with water, and in Joel 3. Here again we find a contrast between Israel's sin-ful history down to the present and its future as the Servant of the Lord.

44:6-23 The futility of idols. The comparison of Yahweh with the other gods begins by touching on some themes that are now familiar. Yahweh alone

their precious works are of no avail, as they themselves give witness. To their shame, they neither see nor know anything; and they are more deaf than men are. ¹⁰Indeed, all the associates of anyone who forms a god, or casts an idol to no purpose, will be put to shame; ¹¹they will all assemble and stand forth, to be reduced to fear and shame.

¹²The smith fashions an iron image, works it over the coals, shapes it with hammers, and forges it with his strong arm. He is hungry and weak, drinks no water and becomes exhausted.

¹³The carpenter stretches a line and marks with a stylus the outline of an idol. He shapes it with a plane and measures it off with a compass, making it like a man in appearance and dignity, to occupy a shrine. ¹⁴He cuts down cedars, takes a holm or an oak, and lays hold of other trees of the forest, which the Lord had planted and the rain made grow ¹⁵to serve man for fuel. With a part of their wood he warms himself, or makes a fire for baking bread; but with another part he makes a god which he adores, an idol which he worships. ¹⁶Half of it he burns in the fire, and on its embers he roasts his meat; he eats what he has roasted until he is full, and then warms himself and says, "Ah! I am warm, I feel the fire." ¹⁷Of what remains he makes a god, his idol, and prostrate before it in worship, he implores it, "Rescue me, for you are my god."

¹⁸The idols have neither knowledge nor reason; their eyes are coated so that they cannot see, and their hearts so that they cannot understand. ¹⁹Yet he does not reflect, nor have the intelligence and sense to say, "Half of the wood I burned in the fire, and on its embers I baked bread and roasted meat which I ate. Shall I then make an abomination out of the rest, or worship a block of wood?" ²⁰He is chasing ashes—a thing that cannot save itself when the flame consumes it; yet he does not say, "Is not this thing in my right hand a fraud?"

²¹Remember this, O Jacob,
    you, O Israel, who are my servant!
  I formed you to be a servant to me;
    O Israel, by me you shall never be
      forgotten:
²²I have brushed away your offenses like a
      cloud,
    your sins like a mist;
    return to me, for I have redeemed
      you.
²³Raise a glad cry, you heavens: the LORD
      has done this;
    shout, you depths of the earth.

can predict events, and Israel is Yahweh's witness. The passage continues with a scathing attack on idolatry. The prophet is engaging in polemics. He is not attempting to give a sympathetic or even fair presentation of the idol-makers. The idol is only a piece of wood, such as one burns in the fire. It can have no power to save. Of course, the pagans probably looked on their idols much as Roman Catholics have looked on statues of saints—not as the actual sources of power but as representations that are helpful to the worshiper's imagination. The point of the polemic, however, is that the pagan gods are fittingly represented by pieces of wood, because they have no more power than their idols. The God of Israel, by contrast, is represented by a living people, whose resurgence from the Exile witnesses to God's vitality.

The polemic against the idols, then, culminates in the contrast with Israel, whom God has formed to God's own glory. Israel is not an icon but a Servant, a living representative. The "fashioning" of Israel entails wiping

Break forth, you mountains, into song,
you forest, with all your trees.
For the LORD has redeemed Jacob,
and shows his glory through Israel.

Cyrus, Anointed of the Lord, Liberator of Israel

²⁴Thus says the LORD, your redeemer,
who formed you from the womb:
I am the LORD, who made all things,
who alone stretched out the heavens;
when I spread out the earth, who was
with me?
²⁵It is I who bring to nought the omens of
liars,
who make fools of diviners;
I turn wise men back
and make their knowledge foolish.
²⁶It is I who confirm the words of my servants,
I carry out the plan announced by my
messengers;
I say to Jerusalem: Be inhabited;
to the cities of Judah: Be rebuilt;
I will raise up their ruins.
²⁷It is I who said to the deep: Be dry;
I will dry up your wellsprings.

²⁸I say of Cyrus: My shepherd,
who fulfills my every wish;
He shall say of Jerusalem, "Let her be rebuilt,"
and of the temple, "Let its foundations be laid."

45 ¹Thus says the LORD to his
anointed, Cyrus,
whose right hand I grasp,
Subduing nations before him,
and making kings run in his service,
Opening doors before him
and leaving the gates unbarred:
²I will go before you
and level the mountains;
Bronze doors I will shatter,
and iron bars I will snap.
³I will give you treasures out of the darkness,
and riches that have been hidden
away,
That you may know that I am the LORD,
the God of Israel, who calls you by
your name.
⁴For the sake of Jacob, my servant,
of Israel my chosen one,
I have called you by your name,

out its sin and redeeming it. The liberation from the Exile, then, is the occasion when Israel is to be remade into an appropriate reflection of the glory of God.

44:24–45:13 The Persian messiah. The central contention of this oracle is that Yahweh is creator of all, and therefore the fall of Babylon and the rise of Persia are God's work. The prophet's primary purpose is not to convince the Gentiles of this but to convince the Jews. So he begins by affirming that Yahweh is the redeemer of Israel and by highlighting the restoration of Jerusalem and Judah. The novelty of this passage, however, is the explicit statement that the decree to rebuild Jerusalem will come through the mouth of Cyrus, who is God's anointed king, or messiah (45:1).

The idea that God's purposes are achieved through pagan kings is not a new one. Isaiah of Jerusalem had said that Assyria was the rod of Yahweh's anger (Isa 10:5). Jeremiah declared the Babylonian king Nebuchadnezzar to be the servant of God (Jer 27:6). Unlike the Assyrian of Isa 10, Cyrus is not accused of pride or arrogance. He fulfills every wish of God. One purpose of his mission is that he himself may come to know that Yah-

giving you a title, though you knew
me not.

⁵I am the LORD and there is no other,
there is no God besides me.

It is I who arm you, though you know
me not,

⁶ so that toward the rising and the setting of the sun

men may know that there is none
besides me.

I am the LORD, there is no other;

⁷ I form the light, and create the darkness,

I make well-being and create woe;
I, the LORD, do all these things.

⁸Let justice descend, O heavens, like dew
from above,

like gentle rain let the skies drop it
down.

Let the earth open and salvation bud
forth;

let justice also spring up!
I, the LORD, have created this.

⁹Woe to him who contends with his
Maker;

a potsherd among potsherds of the
earth!

Dare the clay say to its modeler, "What
are you doing?"

or "What you are making has no
hands"?

¹⁰Woe to him who asks a father, "What
are you begetting?"

or a woman, "What are you giving
birth to?"

¹¹Thus says the LORD,
the Holy One of Israel, his maker:

You question me about my children,
or prescribe the work of my hands for
me!

¹²It was I who made the earth
and created mankind upon it;

It was my hands that stretched out the
heavens;

I gave the order to all their host.

¹³It was I who stirred up one for the
triumph of justice;

all his ways I make level.

He shall rebuild my city
and let my exiles go free

weh is God. The prophet is preaching here a thorough universalism. Pagans may serve Yahweh even though they do not know the God of Israel. Ultimately Yahweh must be known from the rising of the sun to its setting (compare Mal 1:11).

The basis for this universalism is a thorough monotheism, which emerges here more clearly than in any earlier biblical book. There is no God beside Yahweh. Persian religion was dualistic: there was a god of light, responsible for the good, and a god of darkness, responsible for evil. Second Isaiah holds that one God creates both light and darkness, good and evil (45:7). (Compare the rugged insistence of Amos 3:6 that if evil befalls a city, Yahweh must have caused it.) The evil that befell Jerusalem was Yahweh's work; so now it is the rise of Cyrus that brings its restoration.

Not all the Jewish exiles could so readily accept a Persian messiah. The "woes" of verses 9-10 are addressed to those doubters who question whether this can be the work of God. All humankind is created by God and counts as children of God (v. 11). Yet, Second Isaiah has by no means abandoned the special place of Israel. The hand of God can be seen in Cyrus' career because he liberates the Jews and mandates the rebuilding of Jerusalem. It

Without price or ransom,
   says the LORD of hosts.
14   Thus says the LORD:
The earnings of Egypt, the gain of
   Ethiopia,
   and the Sabeans, tall of stature,
Shall come over to you and belong to
   you;
   they shall follow you, coming in
   chains.
Before you they shall fall prostrate,
   saying in prayer:
'With you only is God, and nowhere
   else;
   the gods are nought.
15Truly with you God is hidden,
   the God of Israel, the savior!
16Those are put to shame and disgrace
   who vent their anger against him;

Those go in disgrace
   who carve images.
17Israel, you are saved by the LORD,
   saved forever!
You shall never be put to shame or disgrace
   in future ages."
18   For thus says the LORD,
The creator of the heavens,
   who is God,
The designer and maker of the earth
   who established it,
Not creating it to be a waste,
   but designing it to be lived in:
I am the LORD, and there is no other.
19   I have not spoken from hiding
   nor from some dark place of the
   earth,
And I have not said to the descendants

is for the sake of Jacob that Cyrus is called (v. 4). It is in the interest of the Jews themselves to accept the Persian sovereignty as the work of their God.

45:14-25 The hidden God. Nations may serve God without knowing it, but Second Isaiah believed that the time had come for universal recognition. People from the ends of the earth would bring gifts to the temple in Jerusalem. Verses 14-17 formulate a confession for these Gentiles. Verse 15 can also be translated "You are a God who hides yourself." The point is that until now the Gentiles would not have suspected that Yahweh controls all history. What has been hidden, however, is now made manifest. Yet the notion of a hidden God is important. What is going on in history may not always be obvious. We should not jump to conclusions because one party is prospering for a time while another is down; we must wait and see how things come out in the end. The prophet assumes that the humiliation of Israel was temporary and is now over. Its exaltation, which is now beginning, will be lasting and definitive.

The Gentiles say that Yahweh was a hidden God. Yet Yahweh protests that the word of God was not spoken in hiding but in the Jerusalem temple, the sacred space that is the very opposite of an empty waste. The predictions to which Second Isaiah repeatedly refers are the claims traditionally made in the Jerusalem cult that Yahweh is king of all the earth (compare Psalms 93, 96–100). Yahweh has been hidden from the Gentiles only because they have not sought God in the right place. Now, claims the prophet, they are like fugitives from a battle, forced to acknowledge Yahweh by the course of events.

of Jacob,
"Look for me in an empty waste."
I, the LORD, promise justice,
I foretell what is right.
²⁰Come and assemble, gather together,
you fugitives from among the gen-
tiles!
They are without knowledge who bear
wooden idols
and pray to gods that cannot save.
²¹Come here and declare
in counsel together:
Who announced this from the beginning
and foretold it from of old?
Was it not I, the LORD,
besides whom there is no other God?
There is no just and saving God but
me.
²²Turn to me and be safe,
all you ends of the earth,
for I am God; there is no other!
²³By myself I swear,
uttering my just decree
and my unalterable word:
To me every knee shall bend;
by me every tongue shall swear,
²⁴Saying, "Only in the LORD
are just deeds and power.
Before him in shame shall come
all who vent their anger against him.

²⁵In the LORD shall be the vindication and
the glory
of all the descendants of Israel."

The Gods of Babylon

46 ¹ Bel bows down, Nebo stoops,
their idols are upon beasts and
cattle;
They must be borne up on shoulders,
carried as burdens by the weary.
²They stoop and bow down together;
unable to save those who bear them,
they too go into captivity.
³Hear me, O house of Jacob,
all who remain of the house of Israel,
My burden since your birth,
whom I have carried from your
infancy.
⁴Even to your old age I am the same,
even when your hair is gray I will
bear you;
It is I who have done this, I who will
continue,
and I who will carry you to safety.
⁵Whom would you compare me with,
as an equal,
or match me against, as though we
were alike?
⁶There are those who pour out gold from
a purse

We must observe at this point that the prophet's expectations were not fully realized by the Jewish restoration. Other nations did not feel compelled to acknowledge that Yahweh was responsible for the rise of Persia. Israel would suffer further humiliations in future ages. The aspect of the prophecy that has enduring validity is that Yahweh is a hidden God. Only on rare occasions, like the fall of Babylon, does Yahweh appear to be in control of history. The challenge of Jewish and Christian faith has been to wait for such occasions, to affirm that Yahweh is God even in the depths of the Exile, and to hope that the day of liberation will finally come.

46:1-13 The gods of Babylon. Bel and Nebo are gods of the Babyloni-ans. They are being carried on pack animals in flight from the fallen city. By contrast, Yahweh has carried Israel from its birth. Once again, the release from Babylon is seen as evidence that the God of Israel has power over and above the people of Israel, while the Babylonian gods are no more than their wooden statues.

and weigh out silver on the scales;
Then they hire a goldsmith to make it
into a god
before which they fall down in worship.
⁷They lift it to their shoulders to carry;
when they set it in place again, it
stays,
and does not move from the spot.
Although they cry out to it, it cannot
answer;
it delivers no one from distress.
⁸Remember this and be firm,
bear it well in mind, you rebels;
remember the former things, those
long ago:
⁹I am God, there is no other;
I am God, there is none like me.
¹⁰At the beginning I foretell the outcome;
in advance, things not yet done.
I say that my plan shall stand,
I accomplish my every purpose.
¹¹I call from the east a bird of prey,
from a distant land, one to carry out
my plan.
Yes, I have spoken, I will accomplish it;
I have planned it, and I will do it.
¹²Listen to me, you fainthearted,
you who seem far from the victory of
justice:
¹³I am bringing on my justice, it is not far
off,
my salvation shall not tarry;
I will put salvation within Zion,
and give to Israel my glory.

The Fall of Babylon

47 ¹Come down, sit in the dust,
O virgin daughter Babylon;
Sit on the ground, dethroned,
O daughter of the Chaldeans.
No longer shall you be called
dainty and delicate.
²Take the millstone and grind flour,
remove your veil;
Strip off your train, bare your legs,
pass through the streams.
³Your nakedness shall be uncovered
and your shame be seen;
I will take vengeance,
I will yield to no entreaty,
says our redeemer.
⁴Whose name is the LORD of hosts,
the Holy One of Israel.
⁵Go into darkness and sit in silence,
O daughter of the Chaldeans,
No longer shall you be called
sovereign mistress of kingdoms.
⁶Angry at my people,
I profaned my inheritance,
And I gave them into your hand;
but you showed them no mercy,
And upon old men
you laid a very heavy yoke.
⁷You said, "I shall remain always,
a sovereign mistress forever!"
But you did not lay these things to
heart,
you disregarded their outcome.
⁸Now hear this, voluptuous one,
enthroned securely,

The warning to the rebels, both Jewish and Gentile, is reminiscent of Psalm 2. God is established on Mount Zion. From there God summons Cyrus from a far land. The "former things" are the events by which Yahweh was first established on Zion (see Exod 15) and which are now being reenacted in the return from the Exile.

47:1-15 A taunt against Babylon. The taunt-song against a fallen enemy was a convention of ancient warfare. In this case the gloating is intensified by the fact that Babylon had humiliated Jerusalem. Two charges are brought against Babylon. First, there is the lack of mercy toward the Jews. The Exile was indeed a punishment designed by God, but Babylon was guilty too. We

Saying to yourself,
  "I, and no one else!
"I, shall never be a widow,
  or suffer the loss of my children"—
⁹Both these things shall come to you
  suddenly, in a single day:
Complete bereavement and widowhood
  shall come upon you
For your many sorceries
  and the great number of your spells;
¹⁰Because you felt secure in your wickedness,
  and said, "No one sees me."
Your wisdom and your knowledge
  led you astray,
And you said to yourself,
  "I, and no one else!"
¹¹But upon you shall come evil
  you will not know how to predict;
Disaster shall befall you
  which you cannot allay.
Suddenly there shall come upon you

ruin which you will not expect.
¹²Keep up, now, your spells
  and your many sorceries;
Perhaps you can make them avail,
  perhaps you can strike terror!
¹³You wearied yourself with many con-
  sultations,
  at which you toiled from your youth;
Let the astrologers stand forth to save
  you,
  the stargazers who forecast at each
  new moon
  what would happen to you.
¹⁴Lo, they are like stubble,
  fire consumes them;
They cannot save themselves
  from the spreading flames.
This is no warming ember,
  no fire to sit before.
¹⁵Thus do your wizards serve you
  with whom you have toiled from
  your youth;

may compare the indictment of Assyria in Isa 10, even though it was "the rod of Yahweh's anger." Second, Babylon was guilty of hybris, the pride that sets itself equal to God. The boast, "I, and no one else!" (47:8) echoes a claim only Yahweh can make, and is therefore blasphemous. The taunt against Babylon here is similar to Isa 14, where it is called "morning star, son of the dawn," and to the taunts against Tyre in Ezek 27 and 28. Babylon's wisdom led it astray, as the pursuit of wisdom misled Adam and Eve in Gen 2–3. Babylon was famous for astrologers, who claimed they could predict the future by observing the stars, but they have no power to help.

This poem is imbued with a spirit of vengefulness that may be distasteful to modern Westerners. It was fully endorsed, however, in the Christian Book of Revelation, where Babylon is used as a symbol for Rome and is taunted bitterly in Rev 17–18 and contrasted with the new Jerusalem. The vengefulness must be seen in context. It is the outpouring of resentment by the oppressed. It is not love of one's enemy and it is not the noblest human emotion, but it is certainly understandable. The fall of Babylon was a necessary part of the liberation of the Jews. The taunt-song plays a part in rebuilding the self-esteem of a Jewish community that had been humiliated by Babylon. It can still strike a sympathetic cord with any people who are oppressed by an arrogant overlord and whose resentment is too deep to be glossed over by professions of charity.

Each wanders his own way,
with none to save you.

Exhortations to the Exiles

48 ¹Hear this, O house of Jacob
called by the name Israel,
sprung from the stock of Judah,
You who swear by the name of the LORD
and invoke the God of Israel
without sincerity or justice,
²Though you are named after the holy city
and rely on the God of Israel,
whose name is the LORD of hosts.
³Things of the past I foretold long ago,
they went forth from my mouth, I let
you hear of them;
then suddenly I took action and they came to be.
⁴Because I know that you are stubborn
and that your neck is an iron sinew
and your forehead bronze,
⁵I foretold them to you of old;
before they took place I let you hear of them,
That you might not say, "My idol did them,
my statue, my molten image commanded them."

⁶Now that you have heard, look at all this;
must you not admit it?
From now on I announce new things to you,
hidden events of which you knew not.
⁷Now, not long ago, they are brought into being,
and beforetime you did not hear of them,
so that you cannot claim to have known them;
⁸You neither heard nor knew,
they did not reach your ears beforehand.
Yes, I know you are utterly treacherous,
a rebel you were called from birth.
⁹For the sake of my name I restrain my anger,
for the sake of my renown I hold it back from you,
lest I should destroy you.
¹⁰See, I have refined you like silver,
tested you in the furnace of affliction.
¹¹For my sake, for my own sake, I do this;
why should I suffer profanation?
My glory I will not give to another.
¹²Listen to me, Jacob,

48:1-22 Rebukes and exhortations. The oracle that concludes the first part of Second Isaiah is exceptional in the severity of its tone. We get the impression that the prophet is exasperated by the people's failure to respond. Many scholars have questioned the unity and authenticity of this chapter. There are indeed problems of coherence and consistency, but the chapter is held together by a number of recurring motifs (for example, the allusions to "stock" and "name" in verse 19 refer back to verse 1).

The prophet begins by establishing the reliability of God's word by referring to the "things of the past" that were foretold long ago. He then proceeds to argue for the need for a prophet, since he is now proclaiming something that has not been previously predicted. The denial that anyone could have heard of these things before is hard to reconcile with a passage like 45:21 ("Who announced this from the beginning. . . . Was it not I, the Lord?"), but compare the emphasis on novelty in 43:19. It may be that only the fall of Babylon is regarded as foretold, while the actual return is absolutely new (as in 43:18-19, "Remember not the events of the past . . .").

Israel, whom I named!
I, it is I who am the first,
and also that last am I.
¹³Yes, my hand laid the foundations of the
earth;
my right hand spread out the heavens.
When I call them,
they stand forth at once.
¹⁴All of you assemble and listen:
Who among you foretold these
things?
The Lord's friend shall do his will
against Babylon and the progeny of
Chaldea.
¹⁵I myself have spoken, I have called him,
I have brought him, and his way suc-
ceeds!
¹⁶Come near to me and hear this!
Not from the beginning did I speak it
in secret;
At the time it comes to pass, I am present:
"Now the Lord God has sent me,
and his spirit."
¹⁷Thus says the Lord, your redeemer,
the Holy One of Israel:

I, the Lord, your God,
teach you what is for your good,
and lead you on the way you should
go.
¹⁸If you would hearken to my com-
mandments,
your prosperity would be like a river,
and your vindication like the waves
of the sea;
¹⁹Your descendants would be like the
sand,
and those born of your stock like its
grains,
Their name never cut off
or blotted out from my presence.
²⁰Go forth from Babylon, flee from
Chaldea!
With shouts of joy proclaim this,
make it known;
Publish it to the ends of the earth, and
say,
"The Lord has redeemed his servant
Jacob.
²¹They did not thirst
when he led them through dry lands;
Water from the rock he set flowing for
them;

Verses 9-11 appear as a digression that affirms God's motive for action: for his own sake. This motivation is well established in the tradition (see already Deut 32:27 and several psalms and prayers). Despite the apparent scorn for Israel here, this passage lays a secure foundation for the restoration, since it does not depend on human merit. Verses 14-15 reaffirm that Cyrus will do God's will against Babylon. Verse 16 makes an unusual assertion of the prophet's own authority. Just as the word of God has been public in the past, so the prophet is sent openly now. Verses 17-19 follow with an appeal for obedience. Finally, in verse 20 we get the climactic command, which is the real "new thing" proclaimed by the prophet—the actual command to flee from Babylon. This command comes as the climax not only of chapter 48 but of the first half of Second Isaiah. It is echoed, appropriately, in Rev 18:4, where flight from another imperial city is demanded of Christians in the time of the end. The flight from Babylon becomes a metaphor for liberation from imperial power in any age.

Despite the severe rebukes of the preceding oracles, the prophet concludes that the Lord has redeemed the Servant. Israel's status as Servant is not some-

he cleft the rock, and waters welled
  forth."
[22][There is no peace for the wicked,
  says the LORD.]

II: EXPIATION OF SIN, SPIRITUAL LIBERATION OF ISRAEL

The Servant of the Lord

49 [1]Hear me, O coastlands,
    listen, O distant peoples.
The LORD called me from birth,
  from my mother's womb he gave me
  my name.
[2]He made of me a sharp-edged sword
  and concealed me in the shadow of

his arm.
He made me a polished arrow,
  in his quiver he hid me.
[3]You are my servant, he said to me,
  Israel, through whom I show my
  glory.
[4]Though I thought I had toiled in vain,
  and for nothing, uselessly, spent my
  strength,
Yet my reward is with the LORD,
  my recompense is with my God.
[5]For now the LORD has spoken
  who formed me as his servant from
  the womb,
That Jacob may be brought back to him

thing established by its past actions but something that is now being brought about by a new creative act of God. It is an ideal on the verge of realization.

THE RESTORATION OF ZION

Isa 49:1–55:13

49:1-7 The call of the Servant. Here, as in Isa 42, we have a direct reflection on the mission of the Servant. (The unit is often identified as 49:1-6, since a new oracle begins in verse 7, and distinguished as one of the Servant Songs.) The Servant is explicitly identified as Israel in verse 3, yet many commentators have argued that this identification cannot be original, for two reasons: first, the statement "from my mother's womb he gave me my name" strongly suggests that the Servant is an individual; second, in verse 5 the Servant appears to have a mission to Israel, and therefore to be distinct. Some commentators, then, have argued that the Servant in this passage is the prophet himself. The passage is indeed problematic, but there is no warrant for rejecting the clear identification with Israel or for supposing that the Servant here is different from other passages in Second Isaiah.

The statement that the Servant has been called "from the womb" echoes the call of Jeremiah (Jer 1:5: "Before I formed you in the womb I knew you"), and indeed Jeremiah appears in many ways to be a model for understanding the Servant. More broadly, the commissioning of the Servant here follows a traditional pattern already found in the call of Moses in Exod 3:1–4:17. God makes the commission, Moses protests his inadequacy, but God reassures him. The call from the womb is a way of saying that the mission of the Servant is like that of a prophet or Moses.

and Israel gathered to him;
And I am made glorious in the sight of
the LORD,
and my God is now my strength!
⁶It is too little, he says, for you to be my
servant,
to raise up the tribes of Jacob,
and restore the survivors of Israel;
I will make you a light to the nations,
that my salvation may reach to the
ends of the earth.
⁷Thus says the LORD,
the redeemer and the Holy One of
Israel,

To the one despised, whom the nations
abhor,
the slave of rulers:
When kings see you, they shall stand
up,
and princes shall prostrate themselves
Because of the LORD who is faithful,
the Holy One of Israel who has
chosen you.

The Liberation and Restoration of Zion

⁸   Thus says the LORD:
In a time of favor I answer you,
on the day of salvation I help you,

The apparent distinction between the Servant and Israel in verses 5-6 is more difficult. It is not absolutely certain that it is the Servant who is to raise up the tribes of Jacob; it is possible that God is the subject and that the restoration of Israel coincides with the realization of its mission as Servant. The more common understanding, however, sees the Servant as the subject. In this case we must recognize that the prophet has a special role in the transformation of Israel. He has to live out the role of the Servant and persuade the rest of the people to follow him. He and his followers represent the new Israel, and they still have a mission to their fellow countrymen. Isa 49:4 reflects the discouragement of the prophet, which we have already seen in chapter 48. The reassurance, however, is not only that he will be able to persevere (compare Jer 15:19-21) but that the model of Israel which he represents will prevail.

The mission of the Servant is not only concerned with the restoration of Israel; he must also be "a light to the nations" (v. 6), as in 42:6. Jeremiah, too, was appointed as a prophet to the nations (Jer 1:5). The way in which the mission is to be carried out is clarified in the supplementary oracle in 49:7. The "one despised . . . the slave of rulers" (v. 7) is surely Israel in exile (compare Isa 53:3). When Israel is restored, however, the kings of the earth will be astonished by the transformation and will be led to acknowledge the sovereignty of Yahweh. In this way Israel can be to the nations what the individual prophet was to the Jewish people.

Needless to say, princes did not prostrate themselves as readily as the prophet expected. What is significant, however, is the universal breadth of the mission. Israel remains a chosen people, but salvation must reach to the ends of the earth.

49:8–50:3 Consolation for Zion. This passage has a well-balanced structure. It begins with the triumphal procession back to Israel, as in chapter 40.

To restore the land
  and allot the desolate heritages,
⁹Saying to the prisoners: Come out!
To those in darkness: Show yourselves!
Along the ways they shall find pasture,
  on every bare height shall their pas-
    tures be.
¹⁰They shall not hunger or thirst,
  nor shall the scorching wind or the
    sun strike them;
For he who pities them leads them
  and guides them beside springs of
    water.
¹¹I will cut a road through all my moun-
    tains,
  and make my highways level.
¹²See, some shall come from afar,
  others from the north and the west,
  and some from the land of Syene.
¹³Sing out, O heavens, and rejoice, O
    earth,
  break forth into song, you moun-
    tains.
For the LORD comforts his people
  and shows mercy to his afflicted.
¹⁴But Zion said, "The LORD has forsaken
    me;
  my LORD has forgotten me."
¹⁵Can a mother forget her infant,
  be without tenderness for the child of
    her womb?
Even should she forget,

  I will never forget you.
¹⁶See, upon the palms of my hands I
    have written your name;
  your walls are ever before me.
¹⁷Your rebuilders make haste,
  as those who tore you down and laid
    you waste
  go forth from you;
¹⁸Look about and see,
  they are all gathering and coming to
    you.
As I live, says the LORD,
  you shall be arrayed with them all as
    with adornments,
  like a bride you shall fasten them on
    you.
¹⁹Though you were waste and desolate,
    a land of ruins,
Now you shall be too small for your in-
    habitants,
  while those who swallowed you up
    will be far away.
²⁰The children whom you had lost
  shall yet say to you,
  "This place is too small for me,
  make room for me to live in."
²¹You shall ask yourself:
  "Who has borne me these?
I was bereft and barren
  [exiled and repudiated];
  who has reared them?
I was left all alone;

The central part of the prophecy is a reassurance for Zion. Then the prophet returns to the gathering in of the exiles, viewed this time from the vantage point of Zion (compare Isa 11:10-16). Finally, it concludes with two short oracles affirming Yahweh's power to save.

The most striking lines in this passage are surely those in 49:15: "Can a mother forget her infant . . . ?" Female experience, as well as male, can serve as analogy for God. The analogy of the mother is then transferred to Zion, who wonders how she acquired children while she was abandoned. The abundance of children is indicative of the Hebrew idea of salvation—abundance of life in the land of Israel.

The tenderness toward Israel in this passage is in sharp contrast to the vindictive statement in 49:26: "I will make your oppressors eat their own flesh . . . ." The reference is to cannibalism in a besieged city. Yet, even this

where then do these come from?"
²²   Thus says the Lord God:
See, I will lift up my hand to the nations,
   and raise my signal to the peoples;
They shall bring your sons in their arms,
   and your daughters shall be carried
   on their shoulders.
²³Kings shall be your foster fathers,
   their princesses your nurses;
Bowing to the ground, they shall worship you
   and lick the dust at your feet.
Then you shall know that I am the
   Lord,
   and those who hope in me shall never
   be disappointed.
²⁴   Thus says the Lord:
Can booty be taken from a warrior?
   or captives be rescued from a tyrant?
²⁵Yes, captives can be taken from a warrior,
   and booty be rescued from a tyrant;
Those who oppose you I will oppose,
   and your sons I will save.
²⁶I will make your oppressors eat their
   own flesh,
   and they shall be drunk with their
   own blood

   as with the juice of the grape.
All mankind shall know
   that I, the Lord, am your savior,
   your redeemer, the mighty one of
   Jacob.

Salvation Only through the Lord's Servant

50 ¹   Thus says the Lord:
Where is the bill of divorce
   with which I dismissed your mother?
Or to which of my creditors
   have I sold you?
It was for your sins that you were sold,
   for your crimes that your mother was
   dismissed.
²Why was no one there when I came?
   Why did no one answer when I
   called?
Is my hand too short to ransom?
   Have I not the strength to deliver?
Lo, with my rebuke I dry up the sea,
   I turn rivers into a desert;
Their fish rot for lack of water,
   and die of thirst.
³I clothe the heavens in mourning,
   and make sackcloth their vesture.
⁴The Lord God has given me
   a well-trained tongue,

atrocious situation has a positive purpose, namely, that all flesh may come to know the Lord. The repetition of the word "flesh" is significant, and it highlights the condition of humanity over against the power of God.

The point of 50:1-3 is that the rejection of Zion was only temporary (for the metaphor of divorce, compare Hos 1–3). It was not that Yahweh was overcome by any other power. How could it be, when Yahweh even overcame the primeval power of the sea? Accordingly, no one should doubt Yahweh's ability to save.

50:4-11 The faithful disciple. This unit is often defined as 50:4-9 and distinguished as a Servant Song (although the word "servant" only occurs in verse 10). The reason it is set apart is that it is written in the first person, like 49:1-6, and appears to describe the sufferings of an individual, as does chapter 53. The "well-trained tongue" of verse 4 is literally "a disciple's tongue." The notion of disciple may be picked up from Isa 8:16, where the prophet's message is entrusted to his disciples.

That I might know how to speak to the
weary
a word that will rouse them.
Morning after morning
he opens my ear that I may hear;
⁵And I have not rebelled,
have not turned back.

⁶I gave my back to those who beat me,
my cheeks to those who plucked my
beard;
My face I did not shield
from buffets and spitting.
⁷The Lord GOD is my help,
therefore I am not disgraced;
I have set my face like flint,
knowing that I shall not be put to
shame.

⁸He is near who upholds my right;
if anyone wishes to oppose me,
let us appear together.
Who disputes my right?
Let him confront me.

⁹See, the Lord GOD is my help;
who will prove me wrong?
Lo, they will all wear out like cloth,
the moth will eat them up.
¹⁰Who among you fears the LORD,
heeds his servant's voice,
And walks in darkness
without any light,
Trusting in the name of the LORD
and relying on his God?
¹¹All of you kindle flames
and carry about you fiery darts;
Walk by the light of your own fire
and by the flares you have burnt!
This is your fate from my hand:
you shall lie down in a place of pain.

Exhortation To Trust in the Lord

51 ¹Listen to me, you who pursue
justice,
who seek the LORD;
Look to the rock from which you were
hewn,

The portrayal of the disciple here recalls the confessions of Jeremiah (Jer 11:18-23; 15:10-21; 20:7-18). Jeremiah was "like a trusting lamb led to the slaughter" (Jer 12:19), and his pain was continuous (Jer 15:18), yet God made him "a solid wall of brass" (Jer 15:20; compare also Ezek 3:9, where the comparison with flint is used, as in Isa 50:7). The disciple here, like Jeremiah and Ezekiel, is upheld by God in the face of adversity. Moreover, the disciple appears to accept his afflictions willingly, although 50:10-11 may invoke evil on his adversaries, as Jeremiah also did. (Verses 10-11 are very obscure. "Kindle flames" may refer to a Persian ritual or may be merely a metaphor for trying to provide human solutions rather than wait for God.)

The "servant" mentioned in verse 10 is presumably the speaker in verses 4-9. Here again there is some ambiguity as to whether the reference is to the prophet himself or to the community of Israel. The passage makes good sense as an account of the hardships of the prophet, but it could also speak metaphorically of the mission of Israel to the nations. It may be that the prophet and his disciples represent the true mission of Israel, although they meet resistance even within the Jewish community. The enduring significance of the passage is ultimately independent of the historical reference. It paints a picture of the true disciple as one who perseveres in the face of adversity without concern for self-preservation. Christians have appropriately seen a correspondence between this model and the conduct of Jesus in his passion.

to the pit from which you were
   quarried;
²Look to Abraham, your father,
   and to Sarah, who gave you birth;
When he was but one I called him,
   I blessed him and made him many.
³Yes, the LORD shall comfort Zion
   and have pity on all her ruins;
Her deserts he shall make like Eden,
   her wasteland like the garden of the
   LORD;
Joy and gladness shall be found in her,
   thanksgiving and the sound of song.
⁴Be attentive to me, my people;
   my folk, give ear to me.
For law shall go forth from my presence,
   and my judgment, as the light of the
   peoples.
⁵I will make my justice come speedily;
   my salvation shall go forth
   [and my arm shall judge the nations];
In me shall the coastlands hope,
   and my arm they shall await.
⁶Raise your eyes to the heavens,
   and look at the earth below;
Though the heavens grow thin like
   smoke,
   the earth wears out like a garment
   and its inhabitants die like flies,
My salvation shall remain forever
   and my justice shall never be dismayed.

⁷Hear me, you who know justice,
   you people who have my teaching at
   heart:
Fear not the reproach of men,
   be not dismayed at their revilings.
⁸They shall be like a garment eaten by
   moths,
   like wool consumed by grubs;
But my justice shall remain forever
   and my salvation, for all generations.

⁹Awake, awake, put on strength,
   O arm of the LORD!
Awake as in the days of old,
   in ages long ago!
Was it not you who crushed Rahab,
   you who pierced the dragon?
¹⁰Was it not you who dried up the sea,
   the waters of the great deep,
Who made the depths of the sea into a
   way
   for the redeemed to pass over?

¹¹Those whom the LORD has ransomed
   will return
   and enter Zion singing,
   crowned with everlasting joy;
They will meet with joy and gladness,
   sorrow and mourning will flee.

¹²I, it is I who comfort you.
   Can you then fear mortal man,
   who is human only, to be looked
   upon as grass,

51:1-8 Exhortations to trust. The prophet recalls how Abraham was promised numerous descendants while Sarah was yet barren. During the Exile, Zion was as barren as Sarah, but it too will become fertile. Isa 51:4-5 alludes to the oracle in Isa 2:2-4 ("from Zion shall go forth instruction"—the same Hebrew word, *torah*, is used in both passages). The light to the peoples, associated with the Servant in 42:6 and 49:6, is here the justice of God, manifested from Zion. The permanence of God's justice is then contrasted with the potential transience of the earth and the actual transience of humanity. The power and justice of God cannot be judged on the basis of passing circumstances but only in view of the long-term outcome of events.

51:9–52:12 A rousing call. This long oracle is structured by a triple call of "Awake, awake." The first is addressed to "the arm of the Lord," urging God to repeat the wonderful deeds of old. The Bible has no story of a battle

¹³And forget the LORD, your maker,
who stretched out the heavens
and laid the foundations of the earth?
All the day you are in constant dread
of the fury of the oppressor;
But when he sets himself to destroy,
what is there of the oppressor's fury?
¹⁴The oppressed shall soon be released;
they shall not die and go down into
the pit,
nor shall they want for bread.
¹⁵For I am the LORD, your God,
who stirs up the sea so that its waves
roar;
the LORD of hosts by name.
¹⁶I have put my words into your mouth
and shielded you in the shadow of my
hand,
I, who stretched out the heavens,
who laid the foundations of the earth,
who say to Zion: You are my people.

The Cup of the Lord

¹⁷Awake, awake!
Arise, O Jerusalem,
You who drank at the LORD's hand
the cup of his wrath;
Who drained to the dregs
the bowl of staggering!
¹⁸She has no one to guide her
of all the sons she bore;
She has no one to grasp her by the hand,
of all the sons she reared!—
¹⁹Your misfortunes are double;
who is there to condole with you?
Desolation and destruction, famine and
sword!

Who is there to comfort you?
²⁰Your sons lie helpless
at every street corner
like antelopes in a net.
They are filled with the wrath of the
LORD,
the rebuke of your God.
²¹But now, hear this, O afflicted one,
drunk, but not with wine,
²²Thus says the LORD, your Master,
your God, who defends his people:
See, I am taking from your hand
the cup of staggering;
The bowl of my wrath
you shall no longer drink.
²³I will put it into the hands of your tor-
mentors,
those who ordered you
to bow down, that they might walk
over you,
While you offered your back like the
ground,
like the street for them to walk on.

Let Zion Rejoice

52 ¹Awake, awake!
Put on your strength, O Zion;
Put on your glorious garments,
O Jerusalem, holy city.
No longer shall the uncircumcised
or the unclean enter you.
²Shake off the dust,
ascend to the throne, Jerusalem;
Loose the bonds from your neck,
O captive daughter Zion!
³ For thus says the LORD:
You were sold for nothing,

between Yahweh and Rahab or a dragon. The battle with the sea monster was part of Canaanite mythology. It is taken over by the Israelites as a metaphor for the work of creation, when God reduced order to chaos (see Job 26:12). Here it also serves as a metaphor for the Exodus, when God "dried up the sea." The prophet is not interested in verifying the historical facts of the Exodus—"slaying the dragon" and "drying up the sea" are equally appropriate ways of referring to God's ability to overcome any enemy or obstacle. What matters is not what God did in the past but what God is doing in the present.

and without money you shall be redeemed.
4 Thus says the Lord GoD:
To Egypt in the beginning my people
went down,
to sojourn there;
Assyria, too, oppressed them for
nought.
⁵But now, what am I to do here?
says the LORD.
My people have been taken away with
out redress;
their rulers make a boast of it, says
the LORD;
all the day my name is constantly re-
viled.
⁶Therefore on that day my people shall
know my renown,
that it is I who have foretold it. Here I
am!
⁷How beautiful upon the mountains
are the feet of him who brings glad
tidings,

Announcing peace, bearing good news,
announcing salvation, and saying to
Zion,
"Your God is King!"
⁸Hark! Your watchmen raise a cry,
together they shout for joy,
For they see directly, before their eyes,
the LORD restoring Zion.
⁹Break out together in song,
O ruins of Jerusalem!
For the LORD comforts his people,
he redeems Jerusalem.
¹⁰The LORD has bared his holy arm
in the sight of all the nations;
All the ends of the earth will behold
the salvation of our God.
¹¹Depart, depart, come forth from there,
touch nothing unclean!
Out from there! Purify yourselves,
you who carry the vessels of the
LORD.
¹²Yet not in fearful haste will you come
out,

The second call is addressed to Jerusalem. Ezekiel had said that Jerusalem would drink the cup of her sister Samaria, a cup of grief and destruction
(Ezek 23:32-33; Jer 25:15-29 uses the image of a cup for the destruction to
come upon the nations). Now Second Isaiah proclaims that the cup has been
drunk and is being taken away and given to Jerusalem's enemies. We may
note that the image of Jerusalem giving her back to her enemies to walk on
resembles the Servant giving his back to the smiters in Isa 50:6.

The final call (52:1) urges Zion to put on strength (like the arm of the
Lord in 51:9) and promises redemption. In the future, Jerusalem would be
pure—free from the uncircumcised. The apparent exclusion of the uncircumcised here serves as a reminder that the universalism of the prophet is not
religious pluralism but requires the conversion of the Gentiles to the religion
of Israel.

The concluding oracle of this section develops the theme of the new Exodus in a manner reminiscent of Isa 40. This Exodus will not be in haste, as
was the first one. God will go before and after, like the pillars of fire and
cloud. The joy of liberation is coupled with the call for those who carry the
sacred vessels to purify themselves. The return to Jerusalem has the character of a religious procession from the profane place of Babylon to the sacred
area of Jerusalem. There God is proclaimed king, just as in the psalms of
the old Jerusalem cult.

nor leave in headlong flight,
For the LORD comes before you,
    and your rear guard is the God of
    Israel.

Suffering and Triumph of the Servant of the Lord

¹³See, my servant shall prosper,
    he shall be raised high and greatly
    exalted.
¹⁴Even as many were amazed at him—
    so marred was his look beyond that
    of man,
    and his appearance beyond that of
    mortals—
¹⁵So shall he startle many nations,
    because of him kings shall stand
    speechless;
For those who have not been told shall
    see,
    those who have not heard shall pon-
    der it.

53 ¹Who would believe what we
    have heard?
To whom has the arm of the LORD
    been revealed?
²He grew up like a sapling before him,
    like a shoot from the parched earth;
There was in him no stately bearing to

52:13–53:12 The Suffering Servant. The so-called fourth or last Servant Song is Second Isaiah's best known contribution to Judeo-Christian spirituality, and deservedly so. Christianity has traditionally seen here a prophecy of the passion of Jesus. Historical criticism, however, proceeds on the assumption that the prophecy made sense to the people of the prophet's time, whatever further levels of meaning were later found in it. The original meaning is inevitably bound up with the identification of the Servant. Scholars who distinguish the Servant Songs as separate compositions usually identify a historical figure here—often the prophet himself or Sheshbazzar, the heir to the Davidic throne. In the context of Second Isaiah as a whole, however, the Servant must be identified as Israel, although the prophet holds an idealized view of the Servant's role, and not all the exilic community lived up to it.

The significance of this passage goes beyond the historical identification of the Servant. It presents a model of piety which allows that suffering can have a positive purpose. As such it broke with a long biblical tradition that regarded suffering as a punishment for sin. It laid the foundation for one of the basic ideas of Christianity.

Isa 52:13-15 is presented as an utterance of God. It focuses on the coming transformation of the Servant from extreme humiliation to glory. Since this change will be witnessed by kings and nations, we must assume that the Servant is the Israelite nation or someone who represents it.

In 53:1 the speaker changes. Chapter 53 expresses the astonishment of the "kings" and the "nations" mentioned in 52:15. It attributes to them a startling affirmation: "it was our infirmities that he bore, our sufferings that he endured . . ." (53:4). The Servant, we are told, was delivered up to death and was counted with the wicked, although he had done no wrong. His life was given as a sacrifice for the sins of others. The concluding verses in 53:10-12 are apparently spoken by God and confirm this affirmation.

make us look at him,
nor appearance that would attract us to him.
³He was spurned and avoided by men,
a man of suffering, accustomed to infirmity,
One of those from whom men hide their faces,
spurned, and we held him in no esteem.
⁴Yet it was our infirmities that he bore,
our sufferings that he endured,
While we thought of him as stricken,
as one smitten by God and afflicted.

⁵But he was pierced for our offenses,
crushed for our sins,
Upon him was the chastisement that makes us whole,
by his stripes we were healed.
⁶We had all gone astray like sheep,
each following his own way;
But the LORD laid upon him
the guilt of us all.
⁷Though he was harshly treated, he submitted
and opened not his mouth;
Like a lamb led to the slaughter

The statement that the Servant had done no wrong appears to contradict other statements in Second Isaiah (for example, Isa 50:1: "It was for your sins that you were sold."). The contradiction is only apparent. Isa 53:1-10 is not giving a factual account of Israel's experience but is presenting a model for understanding it. The guilt of Israel is not important for this model. Relative to the nations, Israel was innocent. As we were told in chapter 40, the punishment exceeded the guilt in any case. Here the prophet is concerned with the excess of punishment.

The model of the Servant is indebted to the precedent of the prophet Jeremiah. Jeremiah was like a lamb led to the slaughter (Jer 12:19); so also was the Servant in 53:7. More generally, the experience of Jeremiah showed that a faithful prophet might have to suffer to fulfill his mission. As Jeremiah was a prophet to Israel, so Israel is to the nations.

The model of the Servant goes beyond Jeremiah insofar as the Servant is apparently put to death (53:8-9) and yet will prolong his days and see his descendants. The people of Israel were said to die in the Exile and rise again at its end in Ezekiel's vision of a valley of dry bones and in Isa 26. That is also the original meaning of chapter 53. It is not difficult, however, to see how Christianity could claim that this model was again exemplified in the death of Jesus of Nazareth.

The key notion in chapter 53 is that the sufferings of the righteous can bear the sin of others. This idea is based on the analogy of sacrifice. The logic of the procedure can be illustrated by the famous ritual of the scapegoat in Lev 16. Aaron confesses the sins of the Israelites over the goat and puts them on its head, and then it carries the sins off to the wilderness. This ritual is evidently a symbolic act. It can have a powerful effect on the people, but only if they participate actively in it. They must understand the symbolism and intend to express their separation from sin. The mere performance of the ritual will not of itself transform the people without their involvement.

or a sheep before the shearers,
  he was silent and opened not his
    mouth.
⁸Oppressed and condemned, he was
    taken away,
  and who would have thought any
    more of his destiny?
When he was cut off from the land of
    the living,
  and smitten for the sin of his people,
⁹A grave was assigned him among the
    wicked
  and a burial place with evildoers,
Though he had done no wrong
  nor spoken any falsehood.

¹⁰[But the LORD was pleased
    to crush him in infirmity.]
If he gives his life as an offering for sin,
  he shall see his descendants in a long
    life,
  and the will of the LORD shall be ac-
    complished through him.
¹¹Because of his affliction
  he shall see the light in fullness of
    days;
Through his suffering, my servant shall
    justify many,
  and their guilt he shall bear.
¹²Therefore I will give him his portion
    among the great,

The dynamic interaction involved in bearing the sin of others can be seen even more clearly in a symbolic action of the prophet Ezekiel. Ezekiel was famous for his insistence on individual responsibility (Ezek 18:4: "only the one who sins shall die"). He clearly defined the role of the prophet as that of a watchman (Ezek 3:17; 33:1-9). His job is to warn the people. They have to save themselves by their reaction. Yet this prophet is told to lie on one side for 390 days, and on the other for forty days, to bear the sins of northern Israel and Judah respectively (Ezek 4:1-8). In Ezekiel's case, bearing the sin is clearly a symbolic act. The strange posture of the prophet is meant to attract attention, give rise to reflection, and lead people to recognize the gravity of their situation. Only if they do this can they hope to be saved. The suffering of Ezekiel does not automatically prevent the destruction of his people. There is not a set amount of suffering that he can undertake instead of them. His suffering is only a sign to them. Whether they then escape their doom depends on how they heed his warning.

The suffering of the Servant in chapter 53 can be understood most satisfactorily on the model of Ezekiel. The Servant is a light to the nations. The experience of Israel is to catch the attention of the other nations, lead them to reflect on their situation, and realize that they are even more deserving of such punishment. The purpose of the Exile was ultimately to bring about the conversion of the Gentiles. The mission of the Servant, to which the Jews were called, was to accept unmerited suffering in patient fidelity and so to serve as an example for the nations.

The Gentile nations did not react to the Jewish experience in the way the prophet hoped. Yet the model of the Servant has endured. It provides a way of making positive sense of suffering, which is always a challenge to the human spirit. It also suggests a style of evangelizing, not by conquering others

and he shall divide the spoils with the
mighty,
Because he surrendered himself to death
and was counted among the wicked;
And he shall take away the sins of
many,
and win pardon for their offenses.

The New Zion

54 ¹Raise a glad cry, you barren
one who did not bear,
break forth in jubilant song, you who
were not in labor,
For more numerous are the children of
the deserted wife
than the children of her who has a
husband,
says the LORD.
²Enlarge the space for your tent,
spread out your tent cloths un-
sparingly;
lengthen your ropes and make firm
your stakes.
³For you shall spread abroad to the right
and to the left;
your descendants shall dispossess the
nations
and shall people the desolate cities.
⁴Fear not, you shall not be put to shame;
you need not blush, for you shall not
be disgraced.
The shame of your youth you shall forget,
the reproach of your widowhood no
longer remember.
⁵For he who has become your husband is
your Maker;
his name is the LORD of hosts;
Your redeemer is the Holy One of Israel,
called God of all the earth.

but by bearing their burdens and setting an example. For Christians this model
was intensified by the example of Jesus, whose suffering and death were also
understood as a sacrifice for the sins of others.

54:1-7 A promise to Zion. The prophet resumes the joyful proclamation
to Zion that was the theme of Isa 52:1-12. Two motifs are especially important here. First, Zion is the wife of God. The prophet Hosea used this
metaphor to great effect and suggested that God was divorcing Israel. Second, Isaiah insists that Zion was only cast off for a moment (compare Isa
50:1 for the motif of divorce). Moreover, the abandoned wife will have more
children than one who has a husband. (This is a favorite biblical theme. To
illustrate how God can reverse any situation, compare the Song of Hannah
in 1 Sam 2.) Underlying the metaphor of marriage is the idea of a covenant,
a binding mutual commitment. The language of marriage, however, adds
an emotional dimension to the covenant and deepens the commitment by
arousing feelings of love.

The second theme is the analogy with the days of Noah. After the flood
God guaranteed the future of life on earth: "Never again will I doom the
earth because of man . . . . As long as the earth lasts, seedtime and harvest,
cold and heat, summer and winter, and day and night shall not cease" (Gen
8:21-22). That promise had been kept since the days of Noah. The promise
to Zion is equally sure. Second Isaiah is reaffirming the traditional Zion theology found, for example, in Ps 46:3: "Therefore we fear not, though the
earth be shaken . . . ."

⁶The LORD calls you back,
  like a wife forsaken and grieved in
    spirit,
 A wife married in youth and then cast
    off,
  says your God.
⁷For a brief moment I abandoned you,
  but with great tenderness I will take
    you back.
⁸In an outburst of wrath, for a moment
  I hid my face from you;
 But with enduring love I take pity on
    you,
  says the LORD, your redeemer.
⁹This is for me like the days of Noah,
  when I swore that the waters of Noah
  should never again deluge the earth;
 So I have sworn not to be angry with
    you,
  or to rebuke you.
¹⁰Though the mountains leave their place
  and the hills be shaken,
 My love shall never leave you
  nor my covenant of peace be shaken,
  says the LORD, who has mercy on
    you.
¹¹O afflicted one, storm-battered and un-
    consoled,
  I lay your pavements in carnelians,
  and your foundations in sapphires;
¹²I will make your battlements of rubies,
  your gates of carbuncles,

and all your walls of precious stones.
¹³All your sons shall be taught by the
    LORD,
  and great shall be the peace of your
    children.
¹⁴In justice shall you be established,
  far from the fear of oppression,
  where destruction cannot come near
    you.
¹⁵Should there be any attack, it shall not
    be of my making;
  whoever attacks you shall fall before
    you.
¹⁶Lo, I have created the craftsman
  who blows on the burning coals
  and forges weapons as his work;
 It is I also who have created
  the destroyer to work havoc.
¹⁷No weapon fashioned against you shall
    prevail;
  every tongue you shall prove false
  that launches an accusation against
    you.
 This is the lot of the servants of the
    LORD,
  their vindication from me, says the
    LORD.

An Invitation to Grace

55 ¹All you who are thirsty,
    come to the water!
 You who have no money,

Here we cannot fail to observe that Zion was destroyed again. On a literal level the promise would seem to be broken. Yet, both Judaism and Christianity continue to affirm that "my love shall never leave you nor my covenant of peace be shaken" (v. 10). The peace must be understood as an inner peace that can survive not only the shaking of the hills but the destruction of Zion itself. The restoration from the Exile had shown that God was with the people even in the darkness. The moment of clarity enjoyed by Second Isaiah would have to be remembered as a witness again in darker days ahead. We should note that the oracle is addressed to the servants of the Lord (v. 17) who continue the work of the Servant in the Exile.

55:1-13 Call to a feast. The invitation to eat and drink resembles the call of Wisdom to her feast in Prov 9. The prophet suggests that wisdom lies in heeding his words and returning to Zion. The feast is identified with

come, receive grain and eat;
Come, without paying and without
cost,
drink wine and milk!
²Why spend your money for what is not
bread;
your wages for what fails to satisfy?
Heed me, and you shall eat well,
you shall delight in rich fare.
³Come to me heedfully,
listen, that you may have life.
I will renew with you the everlasting
covenant,
the benefits assured to David.
⁴As I made him a witness to the peoples,
a leader and commander of nations,
⁵So shall you summon a nation you
knew not,
and nations that knew you not shall
run to you,
Because of the LORD, your God,
the Holy One of Israel, who has glorified you.
⁶Seek the LORD while he may be found,
call him while he is near.
⁷Let the scoundrel forsake his way,
and the wicked man his thoughts;
Let him turn to the LORD for mercy;
to our God, who is generous in for-
giving.
⁸For my thoughts are not your thoughts,

nor are your ways my ways, says the
LORD.
⁹As high as the heavens are above the
earth,
so high are my ways above your
ways
and my thoughts above your
thoughts.
¹⁰For just as from the heavens
the rain and snow come down
And do not return there
till they have watered the earth,
making it fertile and fruitful,
Giving seed to him who sows
and bread to him who eats,
¹¹So shall my word be
that goes forth from my mouth;
It shall not return to me void,
but shall do my will,
achieving the end for which I sent it.
¹²Yes, in joy you shall depart,
in peace you shall be brought back;
Mountains and hills shall break out in
song before you,
and all the trees of the countryside
shall clap their hands.
¹³In place of the thornbush, the cypress
shall grow,
instead of nettles, the myrtle.
This shall be to the LORD's renown,
an everlasting imperishable sign.

the promises of the covenant to David. As the king was a witness to other nations, so now the restored people is to assume that role. The prophet does not anticipate a renewed Davidic dynasty; his messiah is Cyrus of Persia. Yet the Davidic covenant is not broken. It is fulfilled through the restoration of the Jewish people. Such transformations are possible because "my ways are not your ways." Second Isaiah maintains the contrast made by First Isaiah between the power of the Holy One (spirit) and mere human flesh (compare Isa 31:1-3).

Isa 55:10-13 provides a fitting conclusion to Second Isaiah by affirming the effectiveness of the prophetic word. The triumphal procession back to Jerusalem with which the prophet began in chapter 40 is the crowning validation of the reliability of prophecy and the power of the God of Israel.

III: RETURN OF THE FIRST CAPTIVES
The Lord's House Open to All

56¹ Thus says the LORD:
Observe what is right, do what is
just;
for my salvation is about to come,
my justice, about to be revealed.
²Happy is the man who does this,
the son of man who holds to it;
Who keeps the sabbath free from profanation,
and his hand from any evildoing.
³Let not the foreigner say,
when he would join himself to the
LORD,

"The LORD will surely exclude me
from his people";
Nor let the eunuch say,
"See, I am a dry tree."
⁴ For thus says the LORD:
To the eunuchs who observe my sab-
baths
and choose what pleases me
and hold fast to my covenant,
⁵I will give, in my house
and within my walls, a monument
and a name
Better than sons and daughters;
an eternal, imperishable name will I
give them.
⁶And the foreigners who join themselves

THIRD ISAIAH

Isa 56–66

Chapters 40–55 were set in Babylon on the eve of the return from the Exile. Chapters 56–66 are slightly later in date and reflect the problems of the Jewish community after the return. It is possible that they are the work of Second Isaiah, at least in part, that is, if we allow that his style of prophecy was altered by the new circumstances. It is more probable, however, that they are the work of his disciples, who emerged as a distinct group in the returned community. These disciples are referred to as the servants of the Lord in chapter 65. Presumably they saw themselves as carrying on the mission of the Servant, which played such a prominent part in Second Isaiah.

56:1-8 Qualifications for admission to the temple. Only two things are necessary for admission to the rebuilt temple—observance of the sabbath and fidelity to the covenant. The prophet does not spell out what the latter requirement entails. The point of the oracle is to insist that two classes of people, eunuchs and foreigners, are not automatically excluded. Eunuchs had been specifically excluded according to Deut 23:1: "No one whose testicles have been crushed or whose penis has been cut off, may be admitted to the community of the Lord." Some high officials at royal courts in the ancient world had to be eunuchs so that they could be trusted with the royal harem. Some people castrated themselves in the worship of pagan gods. At least some of these people could not subsequently be circumcised, and Third Isaiah does not appear to insist on circumcision as a requirement. "To hold fast to my covenant" (v. 4) appears to be a broad moral attitude rather than a matter of specific rituals, except for the case of sabbath observance.

to the LORD,
  ministering to him,
Loving the name of the LORD,
  and becoming his servants—
All who keep the sabbath free from
    profanation
  and hold to my covenant,
Them I will bring to my holy mountain
  and make joyful in my house of
    prayer;
Their holocausts and sacrifices
  will be acceptable on my altar,
For my house shall be called
  a house of prayer for all peoples.
Thus says the Lord GOD,
  who gathers the dispersed of Israel:
Others will I gather to him
  besides those already gathered.

Blind Leaders

⁹All you wild beasts of the field,
  come and eat,
  all you beasts in the forest!
¹⁰My watchmen are blind,

all of them unaware;
They are all dumb dogs,
  they cannot bark;
Dreaming as they lie there,
  loving their sleep.
¹¹They are relentless dogs,
  they know not when they have
    enough.
These are the shepherds
  who know no discretion;
Each of them goes his own way,
  every one of them to his own gain:
¹²"Come, I will fetch some wine;
  let us carouse with strong drink,
And tomorrow will be like today,
  or even greater."

57 ¹The just man perishes,
  but no one takes it to heart;
Devout men are swept away,
  with no one giving it a thought.
Though he is taken away from the
    presence of evil,
  the just man ²enters into peace;
There is rest on his couch
  for the sincere, straightforward man.

The second class in question is that of foreigners (v. 6). The prophet is speaking here of converts who want to join themselves to the Lord. The point is that people who were not born Israelites can become servants of the Lord. The significance of this oracle can be seen by contrasting it with Ezek 44, which presents a different program for the postexilic temple, according to which "no foreigners, uncircumcised in heart and in flesh, shall ever enter my sanctuary; none of the foreigners who live among the Israelites" (Ezek 44:9).

It is evident that there was disagreement within the Jewish community as to whether foreigners should be allowed to worship in the temple. What is remarkable is that both sides of the debate were preserved in the canon of the Scripture. The authors of Isa 56 and Ezek 44 were both sincerely concerned with the welfare of their community, and both were trying to be faithful to older traditions. The exclusivist viewpoint of Ezek 44 received powerful support from Ezra in the following century and may be credited with strengthening the distinctive identity of Judaism. Christianity has undoubtedly found the inclusive vision of Third Isaiah much more congenial in this matter.

56:9–57:21 Denunciation of abuses. There is no agreement among commentators about the unity, origin, or meaning of this passage. Since it re-

Faithless People

[3]But you, draw near,
you sons of a sorceress,
adulterous, wanton race!
[4]Of whom do you make sport,
at whom do you open wide your
mouth,
and put out your tongue?
Are you not rebellious children,
a worthless race;
[5]You who are in heat among the terebinths,
under every green tree;
You who immolate children in the
wadies,
behind the crevices in the cliffs?
[6]Among the smooth stones of the wadi is
your portion,
these are your lot;
To these you poured out libations,
and brought offerings.
Should I decide not to punish these
things?
[7]Upon a high and lofty mountain
you made your bed,
and there you went up to offer sacrifice.

[8]Behind the door and the doorpost
you placed your indecent symbol.
Deserting me, you spread out
your high, wide bed;
And of those whose embraces you lov
you carved the symbol and gaze
upon it
[9]While you approached the king wit
scented oil,
and multiplied your perfumes;
While you sent your ambassadors fa
away,
down even to the nether world.
[10]Though worn out by your many mis
deeds,
you never said, "It is hopeless";
New strength you found,
and so you did not weaken.
[11]Of whom were you afraid? Whom di
you fear,
that you became false
And did not remember me
or give me any thought?
Was I to remain silent and unseeing,
so that you would not have me t
fear?
[12]I will expose your justice

sembles preexilic oracles against idolatry, some scholars think that this
material is preexilic too. Other read the whole passage as an attack on the
postexilic priestly leaders of the community and think that idolatry here is
a metaphor for a style of religion of which the author did not approve. Very
likely neither of these extremes is correct. The oracles are evidently directed
against religious leaders—compare the use of watchman (as prophet) in Ezek
3:17; 33:1-9; Jer 6:17 and of shepherd (as leader) in Ezek 34. We must assume,
however, that the charges are meant literally. The leaders are at best negli-
gent, and there is widespread pagan worship. (Isa 57:9, which speaks of sending ambassadors to the "king," *melek*, even down to the netherworld,
probably means that people offered human sacrifice to the Canaanite god
Molech.) The people who engaged in these practices were certainly not the
more exclusive faction whose views are represented in Ezek 44 and with whom
Third Isaiah had a different quarrel. Much of the Jewish community after
the Exile was quite lax in its religious observance, as we can see from the
tirades of the prophets Haggai and Malachi, and from the reforms that were
necessary in the time of Ezra and Nehemiah.

and your works;
¹³They shall not help you when you cry
out,
nor save you in your distress.
All these the wind shall carry off,
the breeze shall bear away;
But he who takes refuge in me shall inherit the land,
and possess my holy mountain.

Comfort for the Afflicted

¹⁴Build up, build up, prepare the way,
remove the stumbling blocks from my
people's path.
¹⁵For thus says he who is high and exalted,
living eternally, whose name is the
Holy One:
On high I dwell, and in holiness,
and with the crushed and dejected in
spirit,
To revive the spirits of the dejected,
to revive the hearts of the crushed.
¹⁶I will not accuse forever,
nor always be angry;
For their spirits would faint before me,
the souls that I have made.
¹⁷Because of their wicked avarice I was
angry,
and struck them, hiding myself in

wrath, as they went their own rebellious way.
¹⁸I saw their ways,
but I will heal them and lead them;
I will give full comfort
to them and to those who mourn for
them,
¹⁹ I, the Creator, who gave them life.
Peace, peace to the far and the near,
says the LORD: and I will heal them.
²⁰But the wicked are like the tossing sea
which cannot be calmed,
And its waters cast up mud and filth.
²¹ No peace for the wicked! says my
God.

True Fasting

58 ¹Cry out full-throated and unspar-
ingly,
lift up your voice like a trumpet blast;
Tell my people their wickedness,
and the house of Jacob their sins.
²They seek me day after day,
and desire to know my ways,
Like a nation that has done what is just
and not abandoned the law of their
God;
They ask me to declare what is due
them,
pleased to gain access to God.

The rhetoric in much of this passage is simply abusive. The prophet was unlikely to win over the leaders by calling them "dumb dogs" (56:10) or the like. This is the language of polarization, which presumes that the situation is beyond remedy. Such language can only seldom be justified.

Chapter 57 concludes with a more positive attempt "to revive the spirits of the dejected" (57:15) and seems to hold out the prospect of forgiveness. Even the sinners are souls that God has made. In 57:14 ("prepare the way") the prophet seeks to recapture some of the initial enthusiasm of Second Isaiah. The final verse, however, maybe added by an editor, dampens this spirit of reconciliation by insisting that there is no peace for the wicked.

58:1-14 The value of fasting. After the fall of Jerusalem in 586 B.C.E., it became customary to observe four fast days, in the fourth, fifth, seventh, and tenth months (Zech 8:18; compare Zech 7:5). Third Isaiah denies that this observance has any intrinsic value. He does not object to ritual as such— he complains of inadequate observance of the sabbath. Ritual only has value,

3"Why do we fast, and you do not see it?
    afflict ourselves, and you take no
    note of it?"
Lo, on your fast day you carry out your
    own pursuits,
    and drive all your laborers.
4Yes, your fast ends in quarreling and
    fighting,
    striking with wicked claw.
Would that today you might fast
    so as to make your voice heard on
    high!
5Is this the manner of fasting I wish,
    of keeping a day of penance:
That a man bow his head like a reed,
    and lie in sackcloth and ashes?
Do you call this a fast,
    a day acceptable to the LORD?
6This, rather, is the fasting that I wish:
    releasing those bound unjustly,
    untying the thongs of the yoke;
Setting free the oppressed,
    breaking every yoke;
7Sharing your bread with the hungry,
    sheltering the oppressed and the
    homeless;
Clothing the naked when you see them,
    and not turning your back on your
    own.
8Then your light shall break forth like the
    dawn,
    and your wound shall quickly be
    healed;

Your vindication shall go before you
    and the glory of the LORD shall be
    your rear guard.
9Then you shall call, and the LORD will
    answer,
    you shall cry for help, and he will
    say: Here I am!
If you remove from your midst oppres-
    sion,
    false accusation and malicious speech;
10If you bestow your bread on the hungry
    and satisfy the afflicted;
Then light shall rise for you in the dark-
    ness,
    and the gloom shall become for you
    like midday;
11Then the LORD will guide you always
    and give you plenty even on the
    parched land.
He will renew your strength,
    and you shall be like a watered gar-
    den,
    like a spring whose water never fails.
12The ancient ruins shall be rebuilt for
    your sake,
    and the foundations from ages past
    you shall raise up;
"Repairer of the breach," they shall call
    you,
    "Restorer of ruined homesteads."
13If you hold back your foot on the sab-
    bath
    from following your own pursuits on

however, when it is the expression of a just society. Self-affliction is not a good in itself; feeding the hungry is. Verses 6-7 give a concise summary of the essentials of true religion: free the oppressed, feed the hungry, shelter the homeless, clothe the naked. The prophet anticipates the criteria for the final judgment in Matt 25:31-46, but he is drawing on a long tradition of prophetic criticism (compare Amos 5:18-27, which insists that worship without justice has no value). The problems of injustice were apparently as great in Third Isaiah's time as before the Exile, although we might have ex-pected a more close-knit community after the return (the prophet refers to the poor as "your own" in 58:7).

The postexilic community experienced much difficulty after the return. The prophet Haggai attributed their lack of prosperity to their tardiness in

my holy day;
If you call the sabbath a delight,
and the LORD's holy day honorable;
If you honor it by not following your
ways,
seeking your own interests, or speaking with malice—
¹⁴Then you shall delight in the LORD,
and I will make you ride on the
heights of the earth;
I will nourish you with the heritage of
Jacob, your father,
for the mouth of the LORD has spoken.

Sin and Confession

59 ¹Lo, the hand of the LORD is not
too short to save,
nor his ear too dull to hear.
²Rather, it is your crimes
that separate you from your God,
It is your sins that make him hide his
face
so that he will not hear you.
³For your hands are stained with blood,
your fingers with guilt;
Your lips speak falsehood,
and your tongue utters deceit.
⁴No one brings suit justly,
no one pleads truthfully;
They trust in emptiness and tell lies;
they conceive mischief and bring
forth malice.
⁵They hatch adders' eggs,
and weave spiders' webs:
Whoever eats their eggs will die,
if one of them is pressed, it will hatch

as a viper;
⁶Their webs cannot serve as clothing,
nor can they cover themselves with
their works.
Their works are evil works,
and deeds of violence come from their
hands.
⁷Their feet run to evil,
and they are quick to shed innocent
blood;
Their thoughts are destructive thoughts,
plunder and ruin are on their highways.
⁸The way of peace they know not,
and there is nothing that is right in
their paths;
Their ways they have made crooked,
whoever treads them knows no
peace.
⁹That is why right is far from us
and justice does not reach us.
We look for light, and lo, darkness;
for brightness, but we walk in gloom!
¹⁰Like blind men we grope along the wall,
like people without eyes we feel our
way.
We stumble at midday as at dusk,
in Stygian darkness, like the dead.
¹¹We all growl like bears,
like doves we moan without ceasing.
We look for right, but it is not there;
for salvation, and it is far from us.
¹²For our offenses before you are many,
our sins bear witness against us.
Yes, our offenses are present to us,
and our crimes we know:
¹³Transgressing, and denying the LORD,

rebuilding the temple. Third Isaiah attributes it to the lack of social justice.
In this he was the more typical of the older prophetic tradition.

59:1-21 A promise of divine intervention. Chapter 59 continues the theme
of chapter 58. Lack of prosperity is not due to Yahweh's weakness but to
human sin. In this case the prophet goes on to predict a divine response.
Yahweh would be girded as a warrior, as at the time of the Exodus and the
Conquest. Underlying this prediction is the prophet's faith that God has the
power to punish the wicked and the hope that God will do so immediately,
within the course of human history.

turning back from following our
God,
Threatening outrage, and apostasy,
uttering words of falsehood the heart
has conceived.
[14]Right is repelled,
and justice stands far off;
For truth stumbles in the public square,
uprightness cannot enter.
[15]Honesty is lacking,
and the man who turns from evil is
despoiled.

The Redeemer in Zion

The LORD saw this, and was aggrieved
that right did not exist.
[16]He saw that there was no one,
and was appalled that there was none
to intervene;
So his own arm brought about the victory,
and his justice lent him its support.

[17]He put on justice as his breastplate,
salvation, as the helmet on his head;
He clothed himself with garments of
vengeance,
wrapped himself in a mantle of zeal.
[18]He repays his enemies their deserts,
and requites his foes with wrath.
[19]Those in the west shall fear the name of
the LORD,

and those in the east, his glory;
For it shall come like a pent-up river
which the breath of the LORD drives
on.
[20]He shall come to Zion a redeemer
to those of Jacob who turn from sin,
says the LORD.
[21]This is the covenant with them
which I myself have made, says the
LORD:
My spirit which is upon you
and my words that I have put into
your mouth
Shall never leave your mouth,
nor the mouths of your children
Nor the mouths of your children's children
from now on and forever, says the
LORD.

Glory of the New Zion

60 [1]Rise up in splendor! Your light
has come,
the glory of the LORD shines upon
you.
[2]See, darkness covers the earth,
and thick clouds cover the peoples;
But upon you the LORD shines,
and over you appears his glory.
[3]Nations shall walk by your light,
and kings by your shining radiance.

There was no miraculous transformation of Jewish society after the Exile. Later biblical literature would increasingly postpone God's judgment to
an end-time or until after death. Belief in an eventual judgment remained
vital, however. The hope and concern for justice in this world is an important part of the prophetic legacy and is inseparable from belief in the
sovereignty of Yahweh.

We should note that Yahweh is expected to take vengeance on a segment
of Jewish society, not on foreign nations. Those who will be redeemed on
Zion are "those who turn from sin" (v. 20). We find here a division within
the Jewish community and a distinction between the servants of God and
the members of the Jewish nation as such.

60:1-22 Restoration of Zion. Chapters 60–62 stand out from the rest of
Third Isaiah by their exuberant tone, which is very similar to Second Isaiah.

⁴Raise your eyes and look about;
  they all gather and come to you:
Your sons come from afar,
  and your daughters in the arms of
  their nurses.
⁵Then you shall be radiant at what you
  see,
  your heart shall throb and overflow,
For the riches of the sea shall be emp-
  tied out before you,
  the wealth of nations shall be brought
  to you.
⁶Caravans of camels shall fill you,
  dromedaries from Midian and Ephah;
All from Sheba shall come
  bearing gold and frankincense,
  and proclaiming the praises of the
  Lord.
⁷All the flocks of Kedar shall be gathered
  for you,
  the rams of Nebaioth shall be your
  sacrifices;
They will be acceptable offerings on my
  altar,
  and I will enhance the splendor of my
  house.
⁸What are these that fly along like
  clouds,
  like doves to their cotes?
⁹All the vessels of the sea are assembled,
  with the ships of Tarshish in the lead,
To bring your children from afar
  with their silver and gold,
In the name of the Lord, your God,
  the Holy One of Israel, who has glorified you.

¹⁰Foreigners shall rebuild your walls,
  and their kings shall be your attend-
  ants;
Though I struck you in my wrath,
  yet in my good will I have shown you
  mercy.
¹¹Your gates shall stand open constantly;
  day and night they shall not be closed
But shall admit to you the wealth of
  nations,
  and their kings, in the vanguard.
¹²For the people or kingdom shall perish
  that does not serve you;
  those nations shall be utterly destroyed.
¹³The glory of Lebanon shall come to you:
  the cypress, the plane and the pine,
To bring beauty to my sanctuary,
  and glory to the place where I set my
  feet.
¹⁴The children of your oppressors shall
  come,
  bowing low before you;
All those who despised you
  shall fall prostrate at your feet.
They shall call you "City of the Lord."
"Zion of the Holy One of Israel."
¹⁵Once you were forsaken,
  hated and unvisited,
Now I will make you the pride of the
  ages,
  a joy to generation after generation.
¹⁶You shall suck the milk of nations,
  and be nursed at royal breasts;
You shall know that I, the Lord, am
  your savior,

Perhaps these chapters were written shortly after the return, before the problems that dominate the other chapters had developed. Jerusalem is seen as
the focal point of the nations. The prospect of caravans coming from such
places as Sheba (v. 6) recalls the glory of Solomon. The foreigners and their
kings will be subject to the Jews and be their servants, but they will be wel-
come in Jerusalem and their offerings will be accepted in the temple. The
vision of the new Zion is universalistic in this sense, in contrast to the exclusive vision of Ezek 44. The prophet envisages a wonderful transformation—
the people will all be just, and Yahweh will give light to the city by means
of the divine presence. This vision of the new Jerusalem is echoed in Rev

your redeemer, the mighty one of
Jacob.
[17]In place of bronze I will bring gold,
instead of iron, silver;
In place of wood, bronze,
instead of stones, iron;
I will appoint peace your governor,
and justice your ruler.
[18]No longer shall violence be heard of in
your land,
or plunder and ruin within your
boundaries.
You shall call your walls "Salvation"
and your gates "Praise."
[19]No longer shall the sun
be your light by day,
Nor the brightness of the moon
shine upon you at night;
The LORD shall be your light forever,
your God shall be your glory.
[20]No longer shall your sun go down,
or your moon withdraw,
For the LORD will be your light forever,
and the days of your mourning shall
be at an end.
[21]Your people shall all be just,
they shall always possess the land,

They, the bud of my planting,
my handiwork to show my glory.
[22]The smallest shall become a thousand,
the youngest, a mighty nation;
I, the LORD, will swiftly accomplish
these things
when their time comes.

The Mission to the Afflicted

61 [1]The spirit of the Lord GOD is
upon me,
because the LORD has anointed me;
He has sent me to bring glad tidings to
the lowly,
to heal the brokenhearted,
To proclaim liberty to the captives
and release to the prisoners,
[2]To announce a year of favor from the
LORD
and a day of vindication by our God,
to comfort all who mourn;
[3]To place on those who mourn in Zion
a diadem instead of ashes,
To give them oil of gladness in place of
mourning,
a glorious mantle instead of a listless
spirit.

21:22-27 in the context of a new creation after the end of this world. The
idea of a new creation is also found in Third Isaiah (65:17). The prophet
knew that such a wonderful state is not the stuff of history or of human experience but represents an ideal goal that can serve as a guide for our values.

61:1-11 Good news for the poor. The opening verses are very similar
to the so-called Servant Songs in Isa 42 and 49. The prophet sees himself
as realizing the mission of the Servant. The prisoners in question are the Jewish
exiles in Babylon. The year of favor is the sabbatical year, traditionally the
time for the cancellation of debts and the release of Hebrew slaves (see Deut
15; compare Lev 25). The anointing is probably metaphorical (virtually meaning "appointed"). Prophets were not usually anointed, although Elijah was
told to anoint Elisha in 1 Kgs 19:16.

In the context of Third Isaiah, this passage illustrates again the concern
of the prophet for the poor, a concern that was prominent in Isa 58 and 59.
The importance of the passage transcends its historical context, however.
It presents a concise summary of the mission of a servant of God in any age.
It is a mission to raise up the lower strata of society. The Gospel of Luke

They will be called oaks of justice,
   planted by the Lord to show his
   glory.

The Reward of Israel

[4]They shall rebuild the ancient ruins,
   the former wastes they shall raise up
And restore the ruined cities,
   desolate now for generations.
[5]Strangers shall stand ready to pasture
   your flocks,
   foreigners shall be your farmers and
   vinedressers.
[6]You yourselves shall be named priests of
   the Lord,
   ministers of our God you shall be
   called.
You shall eat the wealth of the nations
   and boast of riches from them.
[7]Since their shame was double
   and disgrace and spittle were their
   portion,
They shall have a double inheritance in
   their land,
   everlasting joy shall be theirs.
[8]For I, the Lord, love what is right,
   I hate robbery and injustice;

I will give them their recompense faithfully,
   a lasting covenant I will make with
   them.
[9]Their descendants shall be renowned
   among the nations,
   and their offspring among the
   peoples;
All who see them shall acknowledge
   them
   as a race the Lord has blessed.
[10]I rejoice heartily in the Lord,
   in my God is the joy of my soul;
For he has clothed me with a robe of salvation,
   and wrapped me in a mantle of
   justice,
Like a bridegroom adorned with a diadem,
   like a bride bedecked with her jewels.
[11]As the earth brings forth its plants,
   and a garden makes its growth spring
   up,
So will the Lord God make justice and
   praise
   spring up before all the nations.

has Jesus read this text, with minor variations, at the outset of his career (Luke 4:17-19).

The prophet is here the bearer of good news, like Zion itself in Isa 40:9. Verses 4-9 repeat the universalistic vision of Isa 60 but add a note of concern for justice in verse 8 and a promise of an everlasting covenant, presumably a renewal of the promise to David, as in Isa 55:3. Now all the people are the beneficiaries of that promise. Further, all the people will be named priests of the Lord (v. 6). The prophet sees the whole Jewish people as priestly mediators between God and the Gentiles. This extension of the priesthood inevitably dilutes the role of the official hierarchy and contrasts very sharply with the program for the restoration in Ezek 44, which assigns a very special role to the Zadokite priests. (Compare the dispute in Num 16, where Korah rebels against Moses and Aaron, contending that the whole people is holy, but is swallowed alive by the earth for his impertinence!) The canon of Scripture has preserved both sides of this debate without resolving it. In the New Testament, Rev 20:6 says that all the martyrs who are raised in the first resurrection will serve God as priests for a thousand years, without distinguish-

Jerusalem the Lord's Bride

62 ¹For Zion's sake I will not be silent,
for Jerusalem's sake I will not be quiet,
Until her vindication shines forth like the dawn
and her victory like a burning torch.
²Nations shall behold your vindication,
and all kings your glory;
You shall be called by a new name
pronounced by the mouth of the LORD.
³You shall be a glorious crown in the hand of the LORD,
a royal diadem held by your God.
⁴No more shall men call you "Forsaken,"
or your land "Desolate,"
But you shall be called "My Delight,"
and your land "Espoused."
For the LORD delights in you,
and makes your land his spouse.
⁵As a young man marries a virgin,
your Builder shall marry you;
And as a bridegroom rejoices in his bride
so shall your God rejoice in you.

Restoration of Zion

⁶Upon your walls, O Jerusalem,
I have stationed watchmen;
Never, by day or by night,
shall they be silent.
O you who are to remind the LORD,
take no rest
⁷And give no rest to him,
until he re-establishes Jerusalem
And makes of it
the pride of the earth.
⁸The LORD has sworn by his right hand
and by his mighty arm:
No more will I give your grain
as food to your enemies;
Nor shall foreigners drink your wine,
for which you toiled.
⁹But you who harvest the grain shall eat it,
and you shall praise the LORD;
You who gather the grapes shall drink the wine
in the courts of my sanctuary.
¹⁰Pass through, pass through the gates,
prepare the way for the people;
Build up, build up the highway,
clear it of stones,

ing a special priestly class. This, of course, is resurrected life, but it presents an ultimate ideal for the people of God.

62:1-12 Reminding the Lord. Chapter 62 retains the positive tone of chapters 60–61, but it also reflects some initial disappointment after the return to Jerusalem. It is necessary to "remind the Lord" because God does not appear to be fulfilling earlier promises. The prophet insists that all will yet be well, because the Lord has sworn. The purpose of this oracle is to encourage the returned exiles to plant grain, in confidence that it will not all go in taxes, and to build up the city. We may compare the oracles of Haggai of about the same time, when he promised that all would be well if they built the temple.

The assurance of a divine oath, or promise, is a powerful motivating factor. There is a risk in such rhetoric, however. If the land remains relatively desolate, the discrepancy between the promise and the reality can breed extreme disillusionment. The prophet was attempting to use the power of positive thinking (unlike most other prophets!) to raise the morale of the people, in the hope that their efforts would be blessed. Even if the result fell short

raise up a standard over the nations.
[11]See, the LORD proclaims
  to the ends of the earth:
Say to daughter Zion,
  your savior comes!
Here is his reward with him,
  his recompense before him.
[12]They shall be called the holy people,
  the redeemed of the LORD,
And you shall be called "Frequented,"
  a city that is not forsaken.

Punishment of Edom

63 [1]Who is this that comes from Edom,
  in crimsoned garments, from Bozrah—
This one arrayed in majesty,
  marching in the greatness of his strength?
"It is I, I who announce vindication,
  I who am mighty to save."
[2]Why is your apparel red,
  and your garments like those of the wine presser?
[3]"The wine press I have trodden alone,

and of my people there was no one with me.
I trod them in my anger,
  and trampled them down in my wrath;
Their blood spurted on my garments;
  all my apparel I stained.
[4]For the day of vengeance was in my heart,
  my year for redeeming was at hand.
[5]I looked about, but there was no one to help,
  I was appalled that there was no one to lend support;
So my own arm brought about the victory
  and my own wrath lent me its support.
[6]I trampled down the peoples in my anger,
  I crushed them in my wrath,
  and I let their blood run out upon the ground."

Prayer for the Return of God's Favor

[7]The favors of the LORD I will recall,

of the ideal, the efforts of the prophets may have borne fruit insofar as they inspired people to work at rebuilding their community.

63:1-6 God the warrior. The mood changes abruptly in chapter 63. The warrior imagery picks up from Isa 59 (63:5 corresponds very closely to 59:16), but the imagery is much more violent here. The violence is directed against the Gentiles, specifically against Edom and its capital Bozrah. Edom, Judea's southern neighbor, had become a major enemy during the exilic period. It is possible that this oracle was evoked by some hostile action taken by the Edomites, although many commentators assume that Edom is representative of all hostile nations. We met another violent oracle against Edom in Isa 34.

The image of God as warrior is deeply entrenched in the oldest traditions about the Exodus and the Conquest (for example, Exod 15). The God of Israel was never a pacifist, although the people are often urged to take a submissive stance. The assumption here is that Edom and some other neighboring states were impeding the restoration of Judah. The prophet does not call on the Jews to make war on them, but he hopes that his God will remove the offenders by whatever means are necessary.

131

the glorious deeds of the Lord,
Because of all he has done for us;
    for he is good to the house of Israel,
He has favored us according to his
    mercy
    and his great kindness.
⁸He said: They are indeed my people,
    children who are not disloyal;
So he became their savior
⁹   in their every affliction.
It was not a messenger or an angel,
    but he himself who saved them.
Because of his love and pity
    he redeemed them himself,
Lifting them and carrying them
    all the days of old.
¹⁰But they rebelled, and grieved
    his holy spirit;
So he turned on them like an enemy,
    and fought against them.
¹¹Then they remembered the days of old
    and Moses, his servant;
Where is he who brought up out of the
    sea
    the shepherd of his flock?
Where is he who put his holy spirit
    in their midst;
¹²Whose glorious arm
    was the guide at Moses' right;
Who divided the waters before them,
    winning for himself eternal renown;

¹³Who led them without stumbling
    through the depths
    like horses in the open country,
¹⁴Like cattle going down into the plain,
    the spirit of the Lord guiding them?
Thus you led your people,
    bringing glory to your name.
¹⁵Look down from heaven and regard us
    from your holy and glorious palace!
Where is your zealous care and your
    might,
    your surge of pity and your mercy?
O Lord, hold not back,
¹⁶   for you are our father.
Were Abraham not to know us,
    nor Israel to acknowledge us,
You, Lord, are our father,
    our redeemer you are named forever.
¹⁷Why do you let us wander, O Lord,
    from your ways,
    and harden our hearts so that we fear
    you not?
Return for the sake of your servants,
    the tribes of your heritage.
¹⁸Why have the wicked invaded your
    holy place,
    why have our enemies trampled your
    sanctuary?
¹⁹Too long have we been like those you
    do not rule,
    who do not bear your name.

63:7–64:11 A plea for God to act. This passage is virtually a psalm and especially resembles the communal laments of the Psalter (for example, Psalm 44). It reflects a traditional pattern, which begins by recalling God's saving deeds in the past (especially the Exodus and the Conquest), acknowledges the sin of Israel, and ends with a plea for mercy (compare Deut 32, which ends with a promise rather than a prayer, and such postexilic prayers as Neh 9 and Dan 9). In part it also resembles the laments for the temple in the period of the Exile (for example, Psalm 79). The prayer that God "rend the heavens and come down" (63:19) has a ring of desperation to it. The main problem in interpreting the passage is to determine why the author was moved to such desperation.

Two verses are especially important for the author's situation. One is 63:18. The first half of that verse is translated in the Revised Standard Version as "Thy holy people possessed thy sanctuary a little while," and this

Oh, that you would rend the heavens
and come down,
with the mountains quaking before
you,

64 ¹As when brushwood is set ablaze,
or fire makes the water boil!
Thus your name would be made known
to your enemies
and the nations would tremble before
you,
²While you wrought awesome deeds we
could not hope for,
³ such as they had not heard of from
of old.
No ear has ever heard, no eye ever seen,
any God but you
doing such deeds for those who wait
for him.
⁴Would that you might meet us doing
right,

that we were mindful of you in our
ways!
Behold, you are angry, and we are sinful;
⁵ all of us have become like unclean
men,
all our good deeds are like polluted
rags;
We have all withered like leaves,
and our guilt carries us away like the
wind.
⁶There is none who calls upon your
name,
who rouses himself to cling to you;
For you have hidden your face from us
and have delivered us up to our guilt.
⁷Yet, O LORD, you are our father;
we are the clay and you the potter:
we are all the work of your hands.
⁸Be not so very angry, LORD,

rendering is more probable than that of the New American Bible. Does this mean that the whole duration of Solomon's temple—about 350 years—seems short in retrospect? Or does it mean that one Jewish party occupied the sanctuary for a short time after the return from the Exile and was then ousted by its enemies? (Some scholars think here of Ezek 44, which makes the Levites subordinate to the Zadokite priests, and suggest that chapter 63 was written by Levites.)

The second relevant verse is 63:16: "Were Abraham not to know us . . . you, Lord, are our father." This translation suggests a purely hypothetical situation—compare Isa 49:15: "Can a mother forget her infant . . . ? Even should she forget, I will never forget you." The Hebrew, however, could be translated more naturally as "for Abraham has not known us." This understanding of the text has prompted the view that the author of chapter 63 belonged to a party that was rejected by the official leaders of the community, represented here as Abraham and Israel. The passage, then, can be understood in either of two ways: either it reflects a bitter struggle within the Jewish community after the Exile, or it more simply reflects the initial failure of the returned exiles to rebuild and restore the holy place. In view of the other indications in Third Isaiah (especially in chapters 56 and 66), it seems more probable that the prophet's desperation arose from conflict within the Jewish community.

Whatever the precise origin of this passage, it is clearly a prayer for a time of despair. Two features should especially be emphasized. The first is

keep not our guilt forever in mind;
look upon us, who are all your
people.
⁹Your holy cities have become a desert,
Zion is a desert, Jerusalem a waste.
¹⁰Our holy and glorious temple
in which our fathers praised you
Has been burned with fire;
all that was dear to us is laid waste.
¹¹Can you hold back, O Lord, after all
this?
Can you remain silent, and afflict us
so severely?

Necessity of Punishment

65 ¹I was ready to respond to those
who asked me not,
to be found by those who sought me
not.
I said: Here I am! Here I am!
To a nation that did not call upon my
name.
²I have stretched out my hands all the
day

to a rebellious people,
Who walk in evil paths
and follow their own thoughts,
³People who provoke me
continually, to my face,
Offering sacrifices in the groves
and burning incense on bricks,
⁴Living among the graves
and spending the night in caverns,
Eating swine's flesh,
with carrion broth in their dishes,
⁵Crying out, "Hold back,
do not touch me; I am too sacred for
you!"
These things enkindle my wrath,
a fire that burns all the day.
⁶Lo, before me it stands written;
I will not be quiet until I have paid in
full
⁷Your crimes and the crimes of your
fathers as well,
says the Lord.
Since they burned incense on the mountains,

the frank admission of sinfulness: "all of us have become like unclean men" (64:5). Even if there is a split in the community, no party can claim complete innocence. Second, when no human aid is forthcoming, the prophet appeals directly to God. It was God who brought them out of Egypt (63:9: "It was not a messenger or an angel but he himself" can also be phrased differently and understood to say that "the angel of his presence" saved them. In either case the point is the same: it was no human resource). The plea to rend the heavens forcefully (63:19) expresses the need for help from beyond (compare Isa 59:16 and 63:5: "there was no one"). The plea is based, not on the justice of God, but on God's mercy; he is the Father of all. The idea of God as Father assures the right of even outsiders and castaways to invoke God, irrespective of their standing in the community. The motif is used in a similar way in Mal 2:10 in an argument against divorce. The fatherhood of God was a characteristic motif on the lips of Jesus, who argued that the one Father made the sun shine and rain fall on the just and the unjust (Matt 5:45).

65:1-16 My servants will eat. The division within the postexilic community is more explicit here. The prophet evidently identifies with the "servants" who continue the mission of the Servant of Second Isaiah. This group is at odds with another party, which is accused of a range of idolatrous practices.

and disgraced me on the hills,
I will at once pour out in full measure
their recompense into their laps.

Fate of the Good and the Bad in Israel

8   Thus says the LORD:
When the juice is pressed from grapes,
men say, "Do not discard them,
for there is still good in them";
Thus will I do with my servants:
I will not discard them all;
9From Jacob I will save offspring,
from Judah, those who are to inherit
my mountains;
My chosen ones shall inherit the land,
my servants shall dwell there.
10Sharon shall be a pasture for the flocks
and the valley of Achor a resting
place for the cattle
of my people who have sought me.
11But you who forsake the LORD,
forgetting my holy mountain,
You who spread a table for Fortune
and fill cups of blended wine for
Destiny,
12You I will destine for the sword;
you shall all go down in slaughter.

Since I called and you did not answer,
I spoke and you did not listen,
But did what was evil in my sight
and preferred things which displease
me,
13   therefore thus says the Lord GOD:
Lo, my servants shall eat,
but you shall go hungry;
My servants shall drink,
but you shall be thirsty;
My servants shall rejoice,
but you shall be put to shame;
14My servants shall shout
for joy of heart,
But you shall cry out for grief of heart
and howl for anguish of spirit.
15The Lord GOD shall slay you,
and the name you leave
Shall be used by my chosen ones for
cursing;
but my servants shall be called by
another name
16By which he will be blessed
on whom a blessing is invoked in the
land;
He who takes an oath in the land
shall swear by the God of truth;

Yet these people claim to be holy and warn others not to touch them. This puzzling passage reminds us of Ezek 44:19, where the Zadokite priests are told to change their vestments when they leave the altar so that they will not transmit holiness to the people. Some scholars read the grotesque practices of 65:3-4 as a parody of the official cult of the legitimate priests (see the commentary on Isa 66). It is more probable, however, that chapters 65 and 57 show that there was actual idolatry going on. The fact that the idolaters think they are holy only adds to the grotesque character of their abuses.

We must also assume that the idolaters enjoyed the main power in the postexilic community. They have now inherited the land. The "servants" are outsiders, who are powerless for the present. The prophecy in 65:13-16 anticipates the beatitudes of Jesus, especially in the Lukan version: "Blest are you poor; the reign of God is yours. Blest are you who hunger; you shall be filled" (Luke 6:20). A major function of religion has always been to give hope to the hopeless. The prophet merely asserts that fortunes will yet be reversed. He offers no evidence for his claim. Neither does Jesus in the beatitudes. The only evidence for such a claim is faith in the power of a God

For the hardships of the past shall be forgotten,
and hidden from my eyes.

The World Renewed

¹⁷Lo, I am about to create new heavens
and a new earth;
The things of the past shall not be remembered
or come to mind.
¹⁸Instead, there shall always be rejoicing
and happiness
in what I create;
For I create Jerusalem to be a joy
and its people to be a delight;
¹⁹I will rejoice in Jerusalem
and exult in my people.
No longer shall the sound of weeping be
heard there,
or the sound of crying;
²⁰No longer shall there be in it
an infant who lives but a few days,
or an old man who does not round
out his full lifetime;
He dies a mere youth who reaches but a

hundred years,
and he who fails of a hundred shall be
thought accursed.
²¹They shall live in the houses they build,
and eat the fruit of the vineyards they
plant;
²²They shall not build houses for others to
live in,
or plant for others to eat.
As the years of a tree, so the years of my
people;
and my chosen ones shall long enjoy
the produce of their hands.
²³They shall not toil in vain,
nor beget children for sudden destruction;
For a race blessed by the LORD
are they and their offspring.
²⁴Before they call, I will answer;
while they are yet speaking, I will
hearken to them.
²⁵The wolf and the lamb shall graze alike,
and the lion shall eat hay like the ox
[but the serpent's food shall be dust].
None shall hurt or destroy

who will ultimately set things right and the knowledge that all human power
and wealth must eventually pass.

65:17-25 A new creation. The prophetic dissatisfaction with the present
is even more evident in 65:17, in the oracle about a new creation. The idea
that God would do something radically new was familiar from Second Isaiah
(compare Isa 43:18-19). The replacement of heaven and earth, however, goes
far beyond the earlier concepts. This prophecy is picked up in Rev 21:1 ("Then
I saw new heavens and a new earth") and is often thought to be typical of
apocalyptic literature. In chapter 65, however, the new creation is remarka-
bly similar to the old one. Life will go on on earth. People will still die, and
there is no promise of resurrection or immortality, in sharp contrast to the
apocalyptic literature. Rather, the prophet presents his ideal of earthly life:
freedom from grief, from premature death, from oppression and exploitation.

The concluding mention of the wolf and the lamb (v. 25) very deliberately recalls the messianic prophecy in Isa 11. Both prophecies are fantasies,
although chapter 65 is more restrained in its imagery. Both provide consolation and relief from the distress of the present. The ideal presented must also
be taken seriously, however, as a portrayal of the goal toward which we
strive, even if we cannot fully attain it.

on all my holy mountain, says the
LORD.

True and False Worship

66 ¹ Thus says the LORD:
The heavens are my throne,
  the earth is my footstool.
What kind of house can you build for
  me;
  what is to be my resting place?
²My hand made all these things
  when all of them came to be, says the
  LORD.
This is the one whom I approve:
  the lowly and afflicted man who
  trembles at my word.
³Merely slaughtering an ox is like slaying
  a man;

sacrificing a lamb, like breaking a
  dog's neck;
Bringing a cereal offering, like offering
  swine's blood;
  burning incense, like paying homage
  to an idol.
Since these have chosen their own ways
  and taken pleasure in their own
  abominations,
⁴I in turn will choose ruthless treatment
  for them
and bring upon them what they fear.
Because, when I called, no one answered,
  when I spoke, no one listened;
Because they did what was evil in my
  sight,
  and chose what gave me displeasure,

66:1-6 True and false worship. The interpretation of these verses has
been greatly disputed. Some scholars contend that the prophet is rejecting
temple worship as such; others hold that the issue is how much importance
should be attached to the temple. The second point of view is the more
probable. Third Isaiah seems to presuppose a temple in other passages (including 66:6). Even Solomon's prayer at the dedication of the temple (1 Kgs 8:27)
had declared: "If the heavens and the highest heavens cannot contain you,
how much less this temple which I have built!" The point is that the temple
must be seen in perspective. It is not the most important thing in the religion.

Third Isaiah's perspective on the temple here contrasts sharply with that
of Haggai, who preached that rebuilding the temple was the primary requirement for prosperity in the postexilic community. Here again, the canon of
Scripture has preserved both sides of a heated debate. The temple was very
important for the morale of the community, and we can appreciate why a
prophet like Haggai insisted on thinking positively about it. On the other
hand, Third Isaiah walks in the footsteps of the great prophets, including
Isaiah of Jerusalem, when he points out the danger of trusting too completely
in an institution and reminds people of the ethical demands of their religion.

The interpretation of 66:3 is even more controversial. The Hebrew jux-
taposes four pairs of actions, indicated by participles: "slaughtering an ox,
slaying a man," etc. These pairs can be understood in either of two ways:
"one who slaughters an ox *is like* one who slays a man" (so the New American Bible and the Revised Standard Version), or "one who slaughters an ox
also slays a man." The first interpretation empties the sacrificial cult of all
value; even a cereal offering is no better than swine's blood. If the second

⁵Hear the word of the LORD,
  you who tremble at his word:
Your brethren who, because of my
    name,
  hate and reject you, say,
"Let the LORD show his glory
  that we may see your joy";
  but they shall be put to shame.
⁶A sound of roaring from the city,
  a sound from the temple,
The sound of the LORD
  repaying his enemies their deserts!

Mother Zion

⁷Before she comes to labor,
  she gives birth;
Before the pains come upon her,
  she safely delivers a male child.
⁸Who ever heard of such a thing,
  or saw the like?
Can a country be brought forth in one
    day,
  or a nation be born in a single mo-
    ment?
Yet Zion is scarcely in labor
  when she gives birth to her children.
⁹Shall I bring a mother to the point of
    birth,
and yet not let her child be born?
  says the LORD;
Or shall I who allow her to conceive
  yet close her womb? says your God
¹⁰Rejoice with Jerusalem and be glad be
    cause of her,
  all you who love her;
Exult, exult with her,
  all you who were mourning over her
¹¹Oh, that you may suck fully
  of the milk of her comfort,
That you may nurse with delight
  at her abundant breasts!

¹²   For thus says the LORD:
  Lo, I will spread prosperity over her lik
    a river,
    and the wealth of the nations like
    an overflowing torrent.
  As nurslings, you shall be carried in he
    arms,
    and fondled in her lap;
¹³As a mother comforts her son,
  so will I comfort you;
  in Jerusalem you shall find your com
    fort.
¹⁴When you see this, your heart shall re
  joice,

interpretation is correct, the problem is syncretism: those who offer the
sacrifices to Yahweh also engage in pagan practices. In either case, there is
a division within the community, and the prophet and his followers find themselves rejected. The understanding of this passage depends on our understanding of other passages, such as Isa 57. It seems more probable that pagan
worship was the issue. The evidence does not warrant the drastic conclusion
that the prophet totally rejected the sacrificial cult.

66:7-24 The Lord's power shall be known. The book concludes with
a twofold oracle of judgment. On the positive side, the prophet points out
how far the postexilic community has already come. Would God have
brought them so far only to abandon them? The prophet cloaks his message
in plentiful metaphors of childbirth and mother love. At verse 14, however,
the negative side of the judgment appears. Power for the servants of God
is wrath for God's enemies. The fiery coming of the Lord resembles the coming of God's messenger in Mal 3:2: "For he is like the refiner's fire."

The conclusion, then, has two aspects. The exiles will return from all the
nations. Some will even serve as priests and Levites. All humankind will worship in Jerusalem. This bright prospect has a dark side too. The corpses of

and your bodies flourish like the grass;
The LORD's power shall be known to his servants,
but to his enemies, his wrath.
¹⁵Lo, the LORD shall come in fire,
his chariots like the whirlwind,
To wreak his wrath with burning heat
and his punishment with fiery flames.
¹⁶For the LORD shall judge all mankind
by fire and sword,
and many shall be slain by the LORD.

¹⁷They who sanctify and purify themselves to go to the groves, as followers of one who stands within, they who eat swine's flesh, loathsome things and mice, shall all perish with their deeds and their thoughts, says the LORD.

Gathering of the Nations. ¹⁸I come to gather nations of every language; they shall come and see my glory. ¹⁹I will set a sign among them; from them I will send fugitives to the nations: to Tarshish, Put and Lud, Mosoch, Tubal and Javan, to the distant coastlands that have never heard of my fame, or seen my glory; and they shall proclaim my glory among the nations. ²⁰They shall bring all your brethren from all the nations as an offering to the LORD, on horses and in chariots, in carts, upon mules and dromedaries, to Jerusalem, my holy mountain, says the LORD, just as the Israelites bring their offering to the house of the LORD in clean vessels. ²¹Some of these I will take as priests and Levites, says the LORD.

Lasting Reward and Punishment

²²As the new heavens and the new earth which I will make
Shall endure before me, says the LORD,
so shall your race and your name endure.
²³From one new moon to another,
and from one sabbath to another,
All mankind shall come to worship before me, says the LORD.
²⁴They shall go out and see the corpses of the men who rebelled against me;
Their worm shall not die,
nor their fire be extinguished;
and they shall be abhorrent to all mankind.

the wicked will burn and be eaten by worms forever, as a spectacle for the rest of humanity. The wicked will not be alive to feel the pain of this punishment. The idea of hell did not emerge in the Jewish tradition until about three hundred years after Third Isaiah, yet this passage is rightly seen as a precedent for hell, because it attempts to describe an unending punishment of the wicked.

The lurid spectacle of 66:24 is a rather unpleasant note on which to close the Book of Isaiah. The idea was surely born of the resentment of the prophet's followers, who were excluded from power in the postexilic community. It expresses their hope for justice, but seems excessive in its prolonged torture of dead bodies. It does, however, provide a powerful closing image for the Book of Isaiah. Much of the book was concerned with salvation on Mount Zion. This theme was repeated in chapters 65–66 and reinforced with the theme of a new creation. The final image does not detract from these themes, but it adds a reminder that salvation cannot be achieved without judgment. The wolf will not lie down with the lamb until human evil is eradicated. The smoldering fire of Gehenna stands as a reminder of the reality of evil and its inevitable unpleasant consequences.

REVIEW AIDS AND DISCUSSION TOPICS

I

Introduction (*pages* 5–14)

1. What were the main stages in the composition of the Book of Isaiah?
2. What were the main phases in the career of Isaiah of Jerusalem?
3. What theological principles underlie the preaching of Isaiah?
4. What is the setting of Second Isaiah?
5. What are the main theological themes in Second Isaiah?
6. What are the distinctive features of Third Isaiah?
7. What is the so-called "Apocalypse of Isaiah"?
8. Which themes are found throughout the Book of Isaiah?

II

FIRST ISAIAH (Isa 1–39)

1:1-31 Introductory Prophecy (*pages* 15–18)

1. What themes are highlighted in the opening chapter?
2. How does this chapter relate to the preaching of Isaiah of Jerusalem?
3. How does this chapter relate to the canonical Book of Isaiah?

III

2:1-12:6 Oracles Against Jerusalem and Judah (*pages* 18–41)

1. What is the significance of "the remnant" in Isaiah's preaching?
2. What aspects of Judean society are criticized in these chapters?
3. In what sense can the prophet claim to have seen the Lord?
4. What sign was Isaiah giving to his contemporaries by the Immanuel prophecy?
5. How would the messianic prophecies in chapter 9 and 11 have been understood in Isaiah's time? Do they have further significance for later generations?
6. What role did pagan Assyria have in the plan of God?

IV

13:1-23:8 Oracles Against Various Nations (*pages* 41–54)

1. What pattern is illustrated by the prophecy against Babylon in chapter 14?
2. What purpose was served by the symbolic action described in chapter 20?

V

24:1-27:13 The Apocalypse of Isaiah (*pages* 54–62)

1. In what ways can the destruction of the earth in chapter 24 be understood?

2. Does the Apocalypse of Isaiah attest a belief in resurrection?
3. What role do mythological motifs play in these chapters?

VI

28:1–33:24 Politics and Salvation (*pages* 62–75)
1. What is the prophet's attitude toward the national aspirations of Judah?
2. What is meant by the distinction between flesh and spirit in chapter 31?
3. Why is Isaiah critical of the professional sages and counselors?

VII

34:1–35:10 Postexilic Oracles (*pages* 75–77)
1. How does the Book of Isaiah deal with the desire for vengeance?
2. In what respects do these chapters correspond to Second Isaiah?

VIII

36:1–39:8 Stories from the Time of King Hezekiah (*pages* 77–85)
1. What are the historical problems concerning the invasion of Sennacherib?
2. What assumptions about religion underlie the speech of the Assyrian messenger?
3. What was Isaiah's position in face of this crisis?
4. How should we understand the episode involving the angel of the Lord?
5. What function does the story of the Babylonian delegates in chapter 39 play in the book as a whole?

IX

SECOND ISAIAH (Isa 40–55)

40:1–48:22 Liberation from Babylon (*pages* 85–106)
1. How is the idea of a new Exodus used in Second Isaiah?
2. How does the Servant in chapter 42 relate to the Servant in chapter 41?
3. What is the mission of the Servant?
4. What is the role of the Persian king Cyrus?
5. What purpose is served by the attacks on idolatry?
6. What is the notion of a "hidden" God in chapter 45?
7. What purpose is served by expressions of vengeance against Babylon in chapters 46–47?
8. How does Second Isaiah attempt to prove that Yahweh controls history?

X

49:1–55:13 The Restoration of Zion (*pages* 106–119)
1. Why is the identity of the Servant in chapter 49 disputed?

2. How does the career of the prophet relate to the mission of the Servant?

3. In what sense does the Servant "bear the sin" of others?

4. In what sense can chapter 53 be considered an interpretation of the Babylonian Exile?

5. How far is the mission of the Servant realized in the Jewish community in the Exile?

6. How does the Servant Song in chapter 53 transcend its historical context?

7. How is the Davidic covenant reinterpreted in Second Isaiah?

XI

THIRD ISAIAH (Isa 56–66)

56:1–66:24 Third Isaiah (pages 120–139)

1. What are the requirements for admission to the temple in chapter 56?

2. How does the prophet evaluate the observance of fast days in chapter 59?

3. What is the attitude toward Gentiles in Third Isaiah?

4. How does the prophet understand his own mission in chapter 61?

5. Why does the prophet want God to "rend the heavens and come down" (63:19)?

6. How is the new creation understood in chapter 65?

7. What are the possible ways of understanding the critique of worship in chapter 66?

8. How does Third Isaiah compare with the other prophets of the time, such as Haggai, in this respect?

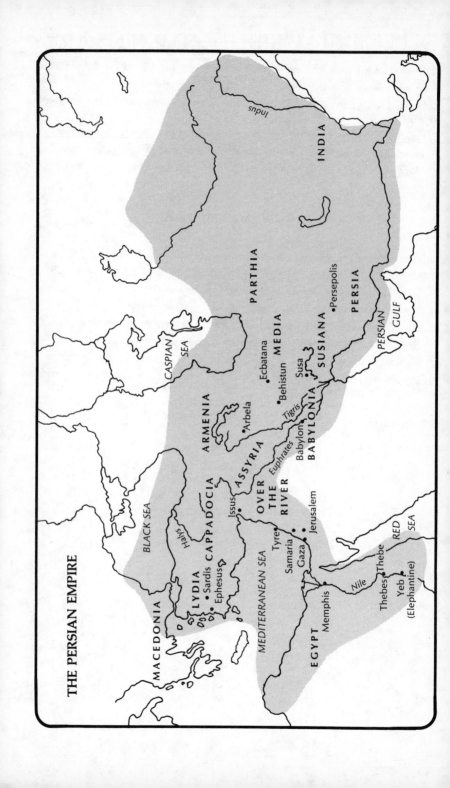

THE PERSIAN EMPIRE